Faith Through the Eyes of Daniel

Reader's Guide on How to Read

by Daniel Johnson

Dorrance Publishing Co
585 Alpha Drive
Pittsburgh, PA 15238
Visit our website at www.dorrancebookstore.com

ISBN: 979-8-88812-071-2
eISBN: 979-8-8881-2571-7

READER'S guide in understanding and how to read my booklet. When you are reading my booklet, And you come across big, bold letters, and different hyphens like... ! ` `` ( ) " WOW!!!, you need to be reading with boldness, excitement, and with some frustration, just follow the hyphens and read them as they're supposed to be, you remember back in school when the teacher I was telling you to read what emotion and to follow the hyphens that are there to guide you in not only understanding but what I'm feeling at the time writing this booklet, You'll get a better understanding on what I'm trying to convey.

Through telling his own story, Daniel Johnson inspires faith and motivation to make changes in your own life. Johnson, as an amplifier of God, reveals what is needed in your life to begin making positive, Godly changes. In his unique writing style, he explains the proper way to read his memoir, with a guide on reading certain words with boldness, enthusiasm, and frustration. Through his style, he forces upon you to read with the desired emotion he felt while writing, which makes for a truly unique storytelling experience.

"This is a Short "Autobiography`` "About Myself" To Show, "And to "AMPLIFIER``... "GOD"...And How Having "FAITH" Will Work For You"... "And How You Can `Pray` For The Revealing Of Your "GIFT"..."HIS" Heavenly "GIFTS"... "That He Will Give You "JEST" For The Asking,``All You Have To Do Is "BELIEVE"``And have All Faith That He Can, "And Will Do This For You, At His "Appointed Time"..."I Am Living Proof Of That ..."For I Testify To My "Accounts"... "To Try To Inspire You To Talk With "God`` And Trust And Believe That Can Answer Your Prayers, "And That He'll Give You "Special" Talents And "Gifts, "To Help You Along In Life. "And How To Recognize Certain Gifts That You "ALREADY" Have, "And Don't Even Realize Yet.(Hmmmmmmm!)

"FAITH"!!! ``THROUGH` "THE EYES OF "DANIEL" "GOD'S "GIFTS "AND "TALENTS …..(Hmmmmm)

"(Hmmmmm) "PATIENCE"… "That's a GOOD! Word" …. "Where would I be, "If I didn't have `PATIENCE`,…."What would I be doing… "Well, "Now! "I know, `To take things "ONE DAY" at a time, "Don't rush things that you have `NO `CONTROL, `Over…"I learned the word (PATIENCE) "So don't "UNDERESTIMATE" this word, "It can be your "SUPERPOWER!….. "You need to learn it, "And learn how to use it, `In a way that it `Serves you, "PATIENCE" IS A "VIRTUE"… "IT come from a "POEM" Called "PIERS PLOWMAN" `Created it In 1360, `` "The "Original "Author, `Of the quote, `Is By "William Langland: "Being both (Useful) and (Difficult), "PATIENCE" is often thought of as a "VIRTUE! "But it also, `Can be "UNDERSTANDING," "Of every "Complexes of "VIRTUE'S, "Including "SELF CONTROL," "HUMILITY," "TOLERANCE," "GENEROSITY" and "MERCY": "And in itself, "There's a very Important Aspect of other "VIRTUES" such as in "Corinthians:1: 13:13 "HOPE, "FAITH, and "LOVE.)" Having Patience, "Is being able to have a "Conversation with a person, "That has a very low IQ, "Or even a "Child talking…. "Gibberish, "Or even a "Person with a "Low "Deficiency,… "Or `Someone of little "IMPORTANCE". "Do you have "TIME" for "THEM!, "Or "Can you give them "TIME? "If you really want to find out how much "Patience you have, "Go up against the very thing that "IRKS" you," See if you can stay "COOL, "CALM and "COLLECTIVE, "And if you can…"You will have learn `Some` "Patience"….."BUT," `You will not have `PERFECTED ` it `Yet, "Even though I `Consider `Myself` an "ADVOCATE" for "Patients,…"I have "NOT" `Perfected` it yet `Either` … "But, I am well on my way too.

`ACHIEVING` this "GOLD," "First of all, "We have to learn to "STOP, "And listen to Ourselves, "Because, "There is an Intelligent side of you,…"You just have to "Learn Who You Are," ("YOURSELF") "To Connect," "And Talk," "And Listen," "To Yourself," and "Don't Worry,"…… "It is Perfectly fine to "Talk to Yourself, "Even sound-Minded People talk to themselves, "Just don't have a conversation with yourself. "When you're "INNER BEAN ``is trying to "RATIONALIZE" with you, "You need to stop and take a listen on what it's saying, `OR trying to tell you," Because sometimes it's trying to tell you some "Good "Stuff……"Now let's talk about another `Attribute that (PATIENT) gives you, "SELF-CONTROL." The Ability to say "YES, " or "NO, ``and "MEAN" IT`… "The Ability to "Control `Yourself"… "like, Your "EMOTIONS" and "DESIRES" or even "EXPRESSIONS" and one's "BEHAVIOR" `` In Difficult` Situations; "Have you ever tried to hold back "TEARS" from a Situation with Family, or "Another" Scenario, "At a "Funeral or "Wedding , "When most of the time "Self-Control, is easier "Said, then "Done,… "Have you ever tried to hold back "ANGER! "I believe this is "HARDER" than "Holding Back Tears,"…"For some maybe, `VICE `VERSA`, SELF-CONTROL, "Will help you all through life, "If you let it, "You can "Activate it at any time," Just by saying the right word, "NO"…or… "NO" words at all,… "I'm speaking about having an argument with someone and "FORCING" on the ending before it happens, (INSIGHT)…… "like "Baseball," "Sometimes you gotta know when to "Slide" or to "let it Slide," "So, "You have to ask yourself, "Is it really worth it , "When you already know the "OUTCOME"…. "let's not be "Simple "Minded about it, "You see it, "Because, "GOD" Has already given you a Hindsight- Insight `` "So, "Why `Add gas to the "Fire, "If that's not what you `Really` wanted in the first place, "Now if you `Allow it to go on, "And add gas to the fuel, " Well then" You, already know, the "POSSIBILITY" that it "CAN" and will "BLOW UP" in your "FACE;…. "YOU" `Can't be in `Control of the "SITUATION" NOW"… "That's why, "I `love to be the "ONE" that has "Total "Control of the "SITUATIONS; `And a lot of times, "After it's over, "And you've had the time to `THINK` about it, "It wasn't worth your time in the first place, "So why waste your "BREATH" on it...? "That's "AIR, taken away from your "LIFE" that you'll never get "BACK," "BECAUSE!! It was a waste of "TIME" .... (Hmmmmm). "And if "TIME," IS of the `ESSENCES ` then why "WASTE" it on "FRIVOLOUS CONVERSATION" that has no "MERITS! "And you probably would end up angering anyway, "So don't waste time with things that don't "Matter, "AND I MEAN THINGS THAT DON'T "MATTER," `So I asked the "Lord" "To let me "NOT" become "WEARY," And "TIRED, "While I'm trying to write this "Book, I only pray, "That I can at "least! "REACH "ONE "LIFE. "At least "ONE" Heart, "Because like I said, "I Hate Wasting Time, "Especially" with "Frivolous "Conversations, that go ``NOWHERE" ``And has no Meaning what's so ever, "So help me "Lord" in Composing this Book, "So that it touches the `Hearts and `Souls of those who are in need of Consoling, "And in need of an" Up Lifting Moment," "l only want to help `SOMEONE,` and not to "MISLEAD "NO, "ONE".... "Have you ever been into a Scenario," Where you would watch it "PLAY out in your "HEAD, "Before it Happen, `We all have the Ability!..."I'm not that special, `Too have been the only "ONE. "A lot of people have done this before, "IT'S like a SIX SENSE, "And lot of people have this Ability, "So with that, Basically, You're looking into the Future (a little bit) a "Glimpse, a `Moment in `Time, It Can `, and "Will; `Reveal itself until You, "If you Allow it to, "And as you know, "With every good thing comes "PRACTICE" you must continue to "PRACTICE" this Treat, "Because if you do have it, "You can lose it,... "Lose IT" , ``BY not "ACKNOWLEDGING IT,".... "It is written that the Egyptians, `Study," And had, the `Ability` to..." Mindread," Ignore Pain," Self-heal, "Levitation," Telekinesis," Hypnosis ``and" Various other things; "MAN! Man! Old man!! "Can you wrap your head around that thought!! and "God" said that He made every `Man `Equal.... "I didn't "Understand back in the day, "when my teacher's would say, "That a

Mind is a "Terrible "Thing "To "Waste, "I found out, "It's very true, "But "God made man `Equal, "He said, "I made Man in my "OWN IMAGE," "SO "IF That's The Case, "WE'RE, `NO "Different from the "Egyptians, "You just have to have the "MINDSET" of the `Egyptians, "And a "WILL to "Do." So when you're in a disagreement with someone, `learn to control the situation, `See it play out In your head before it happens, "I Promise you, "If you Practice it , "You will get "Better" and "Better at it…. `And that's with any, "And every Situation you can think about, "learn to use your "WILLPOWER," "Because learning your" WILL" …" will make you `Stronger and "STRONGER "MENTALLY, "Everybody has a WILL, "It's up to you to strengthen your "WILLPOWER"…"USE IT or "LOSE IT …. "So many times I walked away from an argument with my `Significant Other, "And with some of my close `Acquaintances, simply by `Analyzing it in your head," Before it plays out, "You have the "ABILITY" to do that, "We all do," We just don't "Practice it; "So, yes" We lose "ALL "Abilities for not "Practicing" "Not only lose "Abilities" "But lose "Communication with your "Significant "Other, "Pretty much with everybody, "let me `Explain` to you how this `Can be done." I find myself a lot of time Studying People, "And not for the `Bad or `Good, that might be in them, "But for me…"The question is "WHY," "WHY" this, "WHY that, "WHY" Would a person "DO something like that, or "WHY" would a person "SAY" something like that" and "What makes you Smile" or "Angry; …"That's "WHY" we have to learn, to Connect with your "Inner "Self," With your Inner "SPIRIT, "You can use it as a tool" every human is "Equipped with this "Gifted, "With this `Mechanism` with in them, "Just listen to it, "And trust in it, "let it guide you, "And make sure you or listening to the right "SPIRIT" "Even the word of "God, "Tells us to test the "SPIRITS" so pray for a "DISCERNING SPIRIT" ….1st Corinthians 12:10… "THE Ability to tell who has a "Good `SPIRIT" And who "DOESN'T ,or when I'm in a "GOOD SITUATION ` or "BAD `ONE, `A "DISCERNING "SPIRIT" is what you called it,…"It will take you a long way, (if you pray for the ABILITY) let it guide you along your path in life, "it can save your life one day, "A DISCERNING "SPIRIT" will allow you to look right into a Man's Heart and Soul, "Through His" Eyes," That's why they say to "ALWAYS! "look a Man in his Eyes, "BECAUSE!!! "The Eyes, "Never Lie," So it is Imperative, `That you learn to read a Man's "Eyes." God has blessed us all with these gifts, "But we very rarely use them in life ,"It can build your life, "It can change your life, "With a "DISCERNING "SPIRIT; (for me) "It's really like looking into the future a little bit, "Because it helps you to make Sound Decisions, "like to look up or down, "Go left or right, "Stop or Go, and "Various other ways that the "Spirit" will guide you, "And like I said, "If you don't `Practice it, "You "WILL "Lose It….It was the spirit that was guiding me, "But the more and more I started to know "GOD, "I knew it was the "Spirit of "GOD ``"And his DISCERNMENT SHIP!!.." That's why no one can tell me, "That there is not a "GOD"…Because Beyond a "SHADOW of "DOUBT! "Believe me` "He is real as "Steel" I was fortunate to have found that out early in life, "Of knowing GOD at a young age, "AND GIVING NO DOUBT" And I was also able to "Realize, and "Discern, "Knowledge, "When someone was Speaking it…"I gave my ear to it ,"And due to my "Beautiful "Mother, " MAY" "GOD BLESS her SOUL, "MAY SHE "REST IN PEACE," "While she Continues to help "GOD, to look over her six "Boys and her "Daughter, "Well, at this time there was only `FIVE` of us, "She took us to "Her Church Called, "First "Baptist "Church" And our Minister name was "Rev. "Bobo`, I'll never Forget that "Name" …"I was about ten years old at that time…" And it was from his "Mouth ``,"That I first heard the words, "DISCERNMENT SHIP" And "DISCERNING SPIRIT" and "HEAVENLY GIFTS"…" Mama taught us `All` how to pray and to read the Bible early, "And we were all Baptized by the age of "twelve, "And I didn't know why at the time, "But I `Liked` what the "Preacher, `Was talking about, `He was talking about a "DISCERNING SPIRIT"….. "That could tell me if I was in trouble or not, or "If it was Around me or Not, "" Whether to Move or Not, "I thought that was very "FASCINATING" "And I needed to have that for `Myself!, "I want "ONE of "Those!, "A "DISCERNING SPIRIT" "So I started to pray to GOD for one, "So I could know when I was in the Company of "Good" and or "Evil," "You know what I mean, "Especially being in an "Elementary School" "That could come in "REAL HANDY,"..."SO "I" Started to see it" .."It was Weird, "And see when you're a kid! "These traits are "STRONGER" in you, "As a "Child, "That's why "Jesus said in, "Matthew: 14 (quote) :But Jesus said: "Shuffle, "Not the `little "CHILDREN" And forbid Them "Not, "To Come Unto "Me, "For such is the "Kingdom of "Heaven: End Quote. "So I even started to smell "TROUBLE" When it was around me, "And I had an ideal when there was something "GOOD about to happen from a "Situation, "So, "You need to Pray to GOD for a "DISCERNING "SPIRIT, to control your life and help you along your path, "But! you must `Pray for it, "Because I found out, "What you ask for, "GOD, he will give it to you,... "You have not, "Because you ask not: "And GOD is not an Indian giver, "That takes back, "If He feels," As if you deserve it, "It's yours "If it is of good, "And in his own "Time," BUT!!!!! Even if it's good," Sometimes, "GOD, still may not give it to you, "Because GOD sees what you don't see, "He's able to see further around the corner then you, "So allow HIM to lead you, "With his "Discernment Ship". "This is how I know! "GOD Answers "Prayers `"I Prayed for "THREE" things growing up" And he gave me all "THREE". ... "All the time while I was in Church, "All I heard was, "As prayers go up! "Blessings come down! "So!" Day in and "Day out! "All I prayed for was these "THREE! at this time unbeknown to me, "GOD had also allowed me to see myself in different ways, "And in different Situations, `So coming up as a child, `I kinda knew some of the things I wanted in life, "So with those "THREE things that I was believing in, "Praying and Hoping for was, "FIRST," "A SON, "I wanting a junior, "Someone to call "Daniel Lawrence Johnson Jr. "To start another "Generation, "Second "Generation of "Johnsons, "Who knows, "Maybe start a Johnsonville..."Along with the rest of my Brother's

Children, "And so on, "And so on: And then `I remember traveling one day with my Best Friend, As a young `Adolescent, "His mother invited me on a trip with them, "To "San "Francisco, "That! was my "FIRST" `Airplane `Experience, "And I was "Hooked. I was "ECSTATIC" "And from then "ON!, "I knew I wanted to "TRAVEL!..."Maybe even around the "WORLD".....,"So I said to Myself, (Hmmmmm) "And you know, `Doing that time of age, "What did I know! "NOTHING" "But I knew I wanted to "Travel; "And the only way I could think of at that time, `For me to Continue on Traveling, "Was for me to "Married" a "Foreigner" (Hmmmmm) "SO my "SECOND" Prayer to GOD, "Was for the "OPPORTUNITY" to "Marry a "Foreigner, "That way I would always have a "OPPORTUNITY" `To Continue to Travel, "If `NOWHERE` `ELSE!, "At least, "I knew that I could "Travel "Back and "Forth from "Her "Country to "Mines!, "And from there, "Who knows? "And so, The "THIRD" thing that I started to "HOPE and Believe and Pray for ``was that;..."I would always hear the 'Pastor" preach about "TALENTS `` that "GOD" has given "EVERYBODY" a "Talent" and "Gifts," And I wanted to know "MINE" ... "WOW." TALENT"......., "So what I would do every "NIGHT! and "DAY!, "I would "Pray to "GOD, to reveal to me my "TALENT, that I may know what I am here to do. "Now! my "NIGHTLY" prayers were ... (one) to have a "SON" that I may call him "Daniel Lawrence Johnson Jr." (Two) "That my "Wife be a "FOREIGNER, "So that I would at least travel back and forth, from `My `Country to `Her `Country, "And my (Third one) "I asked "GOD "CONSTANTLY" to "Reveal my "TALENTS, "That "God" Installed into me, "What the Preacher always Preaching about...... "That's why "NO ONE! "Can tell me, "That there is not a "GOD" "ABOVE,..... "BECAUSE All I HAVE IS ONE SON OUT OF LIFE, (Second: "His MOTHER IS A "FOREIGNER," Third: And my TALENTS was Revealed to me,(Well I have more than one) "But my main one is "SCULPTING"... "My very first "SCULPTURE, "If you would have seen it, "You would have thought that I had been doing it all my life," Because when I finished it, "It came out so "PERFECT that you knew it was a "GIFT from "GOD, `like you bought it out the store …(I should have kept that one) "Now, you tell me, "All three things that I prayed for was given to me… "Until this DATE," "All I have is "ONE "SON: "And my "TALENT" has been revealed to me, "And I've "TRAVELED! a good part of the globe, "From having a "FOREIGNER" for a "Wife, "Which allowed me to travel and see more of the states "AND" the "COUNTRY,".… "That I would have never gotten the `Opportunity to `See, "If not FOR "GOD"… "He is good, "NOT some of the time, "BUT all the time, "HALLELUJAH".…, "I've got to give HIM the "PRAISE"…"To you my Father" "Now the Beautiful part about it is "GOD, knows your heart; `All these years of praying and "Acknowledging "Him beforehand, "That he is the "GOD of "GODS, and the "KING of "KINGS," The "GOD, "That Answered Prayers," "let me tell you how `He set it up for me… "Once Upon A Time,…..… "Back in the '80s, "I had a friend name "Broderick White," Well he's a friend to me up to this day, "And as of now, "He still is…"He first was, "And is a good friend of my oldest brother "David, but somehow he became my hangout at "Nightclubs Buddy! lol, "We were hanging out in Long Beach one weekend, At one of the night clubs, "And this particular night, "l meat "Barbara Rogers," It was pure "ESSENCE" I thought, "Saying to myself, "Who is this "Beautiful Lady," `That's before me, `And by herself, `Then I first noticed the "ACCENT," It was "British, "So, "You know she had me at "Hello, "Come to find out, "She was already checking me out,("But Unknown To Me") "She's from the island Of "Bermuda"… "Yeah right!!"Bermuda of all places, "So, We met and dated for about a good eight months, "And we Decided to become "Husband and "Wife, "Well it didn't take much to convince me you know, "Because that's what I was praying for in the first place, "Now I've gotten My "FIRST" prayer from "God, "TO have a "Foreigner Wife, "Now I know at least I'll go from America to the to Bermuda, a part of "Europe" ``Wow" "Now I'm "TRAVELING!!! "God is Good," "But!" Wait a "Minute! "Let me show how good he is.

"Three years later! "Daniel Lawrence Johnson" `Jr. "Was Born, `You see God heard ALL my prayers, "And now, my "SECOND" prayer has been "Answered, "When I was praying, `From the time I was a youth, `From the age of ten, "I understood what I wanted in life, "What I wanted GOD to bless me with in life, "And he Certainly did give me all "THREE" `"Until this day, All I have is a "Son, "My Wife was a Foreigner, And now traveled more places than I've ever traveled before, And it's all because of this marriage that "God put Together. "God was so good to me in answering prayers, "That even the devil was jealous, "let me show you how he tried to take my Son away from me, "Even when he was in the womb," Here's what happened, "With In six months in my wife pregnancy, "She began to have complications with the pregnancy, "And now, `We are going back and forth` to the hospital, `Until they had to admitted her in earlier then she was supposed to be,..."So in her "Eighth Month"... "One particular time I came to the hospital for a visit, "And the "Doctor comes up to me, And pulls me to the side, And said, "Mr. Johnson, I have a little Bit of Bad news to tell you, 'And it's not good, "So I said, "What happened, Doctor?" "Whats wrong!... "He said, "You may have to choose between having a "WIFE" or a "SON" Because both of them may NOT make it through the Procedure, "Due to her Complications. Now she was twenty-seven years old when she conceived," Which I thought was kinda strange, "Only because, all eight of her Siblings had children already, "And I know I was not her first Boyfriend," Hmmmm, "And it was getting late for her, "But not Impossible, "But you know what! "The devil is a liar, And "GOD is good… You see GOD blessed me with "BOTH" of them, "But I looked at it with a Spiritual Eye, "That she was "BARREN" by "GOD," Until we got Together, "That we may make a child and name him Daniel Lawrence Johnson Jr; "GOD could have gave her A child Long time ago, "With one of her earlier boyfriend, "But he didn't... "Why!! I'll tell you "WHY" "Because!! I Was a Praying Man!!!"And "GOD" Answers "Prayers" And GOD is not a liar, "That same night he was Born... "My prayers to the Lord that night was, Giving all thanks and Praise to you Father who art in Heaven," Because it was you who made this Possible for me to have my Son and my Wife .... Which I prayed for many years, "And to have the devil steal it from me NO, NO, NO, NO, I have my Wife and my Son "Unharmed"....The (devil) is a liar, "So, Soon as I got the chance, "After bringing them home from the hospital, " I said to myself, "That I need to Bless him under the Stars, "And Dedicate Him to GOD,... "GOD! Please! "You take my Son into your "HANDS," whom I DEDICATE BACK! to YOU!, "INTO your CARE,"..."For you to do with him as you Please, "And to use him as you Need"... "I could not have had him without you, "So take Him, And, pour your "Spirit into Him, So that your words will be Written, and Etched into his Heart,... Until this day, "He's is a Anointed `Child of God, "There was nothing I, or his Mother had to teach him, "Because my "Father in "Heaven had took him already into his hands,"The words of God says, Jeremiah 31: 33, I will put my law within them, and I will write it on their hearts; and I will be their "GOD, "And they shall be my "People," "let me tell you, I've seen enough "Bible movies and "Spiritual plays to know, "That you are supposed to "Rededicate your "Child back to "GOD" the Moment "He he or "She is "Born, "AND THAT'S WHAT I DID!!!, "So let me show you how this works; "BY doing that, "No one can do him no Harm, without imposing some type of spiritual curse upon themselves unleashing the very demon that they tried to inflict; "No Wrong, "Because it will come back to them "Sevenfold, "Thank you, "JESUS. "Until This day "Little Daniel doesn't Smoke, Curse or Drink, loves to Help the Poor, " Give them not only "Money, "BUT he gives his"TIME ``,"And loves to talk and converse with them also,..."He understands the needs of people,"Do you have the TIME to give to the LESS FORTUNATE people than yourself. "Daniel is a stand-up guy for the "Lord, "I ain't got a bad thing to say about him, `I don't think anyone does.`Ask any of his "PEERS, "They speak highly of him, "And he's known, "And loved by the Media."He's been all over the Western side of the "World, "And half of the "Eastern Side," "And I know that his itinerary has gotten larger,... I just ant check in with him lately, `He's probably finished with that side already, "And he's still going, "My GOD above has blessed me with him, "So when I "REDEDICATED" him back to the "LORD "GOD, "He worked on Him in a "MIGHTY WAY," "And instilled into Him, "Everything he is "Today, "IT was nothing that we had to teach him, "IT was "NOTHING" no one had to show him, "GOD had his "ITINERARY" already "READY," "Daniel Jr. already knew In his HEART and MINE where he wanted to go in life, a lot of people would say that my wife raise him but "I BEG THE DIFFER," Yeah, "She, played a big part in his "Life, I left him at thirteen or fourteen, "GOD" Raised Him Also," And instilled in him before I left the ISLAND on what and where and how he was gonna lead and live his life, "Because it was already pray for ,Oh" but make no "MISTAKE" I'm not taking nothing from his "MOTHER," "BECAUSE SHE" Provided for him after I left the ISLAND, at that time like I said, "He was about thirteen or fouteen but make no mistake, "GOD already had his way with him and had plans for him, listen, you can't take "GOD'S CREDIT," "Because, from the time I was there with him, "And what I had seen in him before I left, "GOD had already start to mold him,....."My Mother told me one day,"She said, "Son, I can see that you're a wise child in your early age, "And those words kind of stuck with me, It helped me to realize a lot of things about myself," And I saw it in him also before I left the ISLAND, I already knew he was not going to have any problems coming up mentally, "like I said, My mother used to tell me all the time, `When I was young, `That I was a very Intelligent, "And your very `Smart Intellectually` for your age, "And as you know, "The apple don't fall too far from the tree, "I would wonder why I was able to figure out things Sometimes, `INSTANTANEOUSLY, "I would have "WORDS, and "CATCHPHRASES in my mind already, And, I would wonder where they were coming from sometimes, "So, "That's how I Already I knew my Son, "Was Equipped Long before I left the ISLAND, "It was nothing he needed to be taught, "Because, It was instilled in him,

"When he was a baby,"He was "INTELLIGENT," all the way through School, he was "INTELLIGENT," and all through College he was "INTELLIGENT".... "Thanks to his mother for that, I have to give her all that "RECOGNITION, "Because she did that," Sent him to School and College, but like I said, no `School, no `College can give him what GOD has given him. It was already "EMBEDDED" into his HEARTS and SOUL and MIND what to do in life, "Because I was a praying "MAN".... "But now" "Back to when he was born, "I had to go and find work now, "So I get the newspaper out, "And went to the help wanted Ads, (Hmmmm) "And low and behold, "I see a Carpenter's position open for a Carpenter, "Now get this! First of all, "I never picked up a Hammer before in my life, Now, I'm about twenty years old, "And I had the gift to gab, also, lol. "So in the newspaper was Carpenter's positioning open with, "Austin Simon and "John Trott, lol.. "And I remember telling them I had experience in this field of work, "I told them I worked for "Cabinet Masters, in the States, and even "Floor Daniels, one of the biggest Construction Companies back in California, I just knew the name of these Companies," But. "No Experience At All," I lied" Because I needed work, "So I "SAID what I "SAID and it all sounded good, "Because they gave me a job...lol, "But check this; "In Three Days "Mr. Simon came to me, "And said, "Son, "You ain't no Carpenter, "With the serious and straight face..." He said I actually knew that The first day, "When you put the "Jack's for the "Second Deck Upside Down, "I knew then, `You weren't a Carpenter, "But I watched you for a Couple more days, "And made this "Determination... So!!! Like I said I watched you a "Couple more Days, "And you got something in you, "A lot of Determination, "And it's not your Carpentry Skills, "That's for sure, lol, "But I see the "Spunk in you, "You've got Drive, "Yankee Boy" ... "(And that's how I've got my nickname "Yankee Boy)" So the hole company started to call me Yankee Boy, I became known as "Yankee Boy, "Over the whole Island, "Yankee is the name they call all "Americans, "But for me it stuck as a nickname ..., "So Austin Simon came to me, "And said, "If you want to continue to work for me,... for those three days that I didn't say nothing to you, "I'll pay you the Carpenter fee at $12.00/hr. "But from here on out, "If you want to stay working for me, you can be a laborer, "At $8.50/hr. "And that was in 1982; "When in America, minimum wage was $2.85/hr.(Hmmmmmmmm)"And he said," I will "TEACH" you everything you need to know about "Carpentry, "And I said "COOL" Yes Sir, and you gotta remember this is 1982, 83, "When back home, in the States, "I was only making $2.85/hr. at Jack in the Box, I was "ECSTATIC, "I couldn't wait to go home, and tell my Wife Barbara, "So this went on for about two to three years of him teaching me, "And then he had decided that he was gonna liquidate the company, "To become a "Building Inspector for the Island, "So he told us he had some "Connections, "And with the eight employees that he had, including "Me, he hooked us all up with different Construction Companies, "Big Companies too, " His Company was like a, Mom and Pop Company, "So he sent four of them to, `Berlin, `Canyon and `Marie inc. "And four of us to `Sea `Land `Construction, ``To whom I was sent too, "Let me show you how "God" works in mysterious ways, "For a person "Who's Never Had A Hammer In His Hand, "In his life,"And I'm here, `On one of the "Biggest "Contraction Co. and Sites, on the "Island, "And doing things I never thought I'd be doing, "Things were coming to me like I had them written on the back of my hands, "I'm talking about knowing "Dimensions" "Being able Draw, and lay out a floor plan, "I mean all types of "Carpentry Tricks, "With the Solutions, "On how certain things should go, or be Rebuilt, "But within the "Carpentry Guidelines, "The things that I was figuring out,..."I shouldn't have known, "That was nobody BUT!! "God" leading me, "Teaching me, "And you know when "God give it to you, "There's no taking back, "It was his gift to me, "So it was "ETCHED" in my MIND and in my HEART and in my SPIRIT and my SOUL, "It was a "GOD-GIVEN talent, "So the Company; `I guess seen something in me also, "And the Superintendent came to me one day and said, "Daniel, `We send "Two `Carpenters, "Two `Masons, and "Two `Electricians, to School every year, "And so we have been watching you, "And have determined, "That you will be One of the Carpenters, "That we will send you to School for three years," And will "Pay" for it…, "This is how it goes…"You will continue to work for us," You will work a half day, "And go to School the other half, "I was really "Honored" ,"But It showed me that it is true, "What "GOD says that he gives everybody a talent, and that's not all." So after about two years of going to school, "The Company started to lay off work a little bit, because work started to slow down, "So, "Being I was still in school, "And still had another year to go before I finish school, "So they couldn't lay "Me off, "Because, "Basically, I was a Investment: "To the Company, "And I still have a year to go, "So they sent me to the Carpenter's Shop, " To work in there for a little while until things pick up , "And that's where I learned a lot about, Finishing Work,… "So I received four Certificates from the school of Carpentry, One in Finishing, One in Roofing, One in Blueprinting and one in Rough Work…" But one Day!!! I was at work, "And I saw this Jamaican guy chopping wood, "Making a Sculpture, "And I said to myself "MAN" I would love to learn to do that!!!" So I went up to him and asked, "hey" RUDEBOY (in my best `Jamaican `accent) Can you teach me to do that!! "I think your work is awesome, "And it was, "So he said to me, "Ja mon" in his Jamaican accent, "And said pick up a piece of wood," And start to Chopping it, "And what you "See" in it" that is what it will be, "Bring it to life" As you go on,..(seen) another Jamaican term, "That was more than enough information for me to start full blast at it, LOL…, "So I picked up a log of wood, "And it had two branches on it, "One on each side of the wood log…. "When I finished in three months, it was an African, "Holding a shield, "That had the words on the bottom of the stump, "Freedom" was carved in It," A Masterpiece, I mean, A very, Detailed Piece, "You would have thought that I had been doing this all my life…(Hmmmmm) I mean down to the detail, "How could this be, "Then I knew again it was "GOD"… "GOD" has shown me not one, "But two of my Talents: "Carpentry" and "Sculpturing," God's Good All The Time… "That's why I continue to give "GOD"all the praise, "Because from the time of young, "I Started to pray for three "SPECIFIC" things, "And he's gave me all "THREE" and more, I "Prayed" for a Son, "And all I have is a "Son," I "Prayed for my "TALENT" to be "Revealed," "And he Revealed it to me, not one but, Two different TALENTS! I "Prayed for my "Wife" to be a "Foreigner" `So I could travel, "And low and "Behold," "She's from "Bermuda". "She and my "Son are what they call "British Subjects" "Wow!!! "Can you believe that, "All Three of Them," "And I "Believe" I may have found another "ONE," "He did Say, "That he gives us "MANY" TALENTS," I'm trying to perfect the new one I just stumbled upon… "I Believe I have the gift to speak, "Because I talk too much, and "GOD doesn't make "Mistakes." People just don't realize there's a reason for everything under the sun, "Ecclesiastes 3:1 "To everything there is a Season"… "So you need to analyze yourself, "And see yourself for who you really are, "Don't sell yourself short," Know your worth, "GOD doesn't make "Mistakes" `I said …,"God said to know thyself; "And for all of those people out there who talk too much "You need to realize and pay "ATTENTION," It's not by "Chance," or "Mistake," "You have to learn how to "HARNESS" your gifts, "learn to use it in a "Positive" way," SPEAK"!!! It is also a "Talent," "MR. PREACHER"!!!,   "TEACHER"!!!, "SPEAKER"!!!,"MOTIVATIONAL SPEAKER"!!! "Should I go on?" Come on now" I know someone here's me, "What I'm trying to say is, "You got to have figured this out sooner or later, "Now I know this in my older days, "This is why I'm trying to "ENLIGHTEN" as many young people as I can,"So they can learn early, "And know how, "To not waste time, "As I did in my younger Days. "If you already "Believe in "God," "And the "Powers of "God," "You are more than halfway there, "He is real, "I am living proof! "Because, a "Doctor also! "Told my "Mother, "That I might not make it,"From the "Operating" "Table," `You see I had a major operation at the age of thirteen, "On my "Colon, "The large Intestine was infected, "It was something that ran in the family I was told, "I was actually "Dying on my way to the "Hospital,"

And I didn't even know it, "My Mother took me to the "First "Hospital, "Because, I was complaining of stomach pain, "Well, the "Doctor at that "Hospital," "Told" Her to rush me straight to "Children" "Memorial" "Hospital" In "Hollywood," `Is where I went through; A nine-hour Surgery, "As soon as I got there;" They were already set and ready; "To "Start the "Operation" "Procedure" Right "AWAY." "Doing this "Operation, "I lost "Eight "Pints "Of "Blood, "And as soon as the "Doctor "Finished, "He came out and told my "Mother," "It is in "GOD'S hands now, "And that I had a 50/50 "Chance of "Survival, "I remember them telling me, `After the Surgery`, "That I was a strong "Young Man," "little did he know my "WILL" was "STRONGER" in "GOD," But that devil tried to take me,... "And then he tried to take my "Son"... "Now that's one of the things that makes you "Say (Hmmmmm) is all about, "So what is the devil's mission, "I ask myself… "Because he's tried twice in my family tree, "In my "Name… "With me, and then my "Son, "What is he trying to do? "There's one thing I know," And two thing's for sure, the devil can't touch "Me nor my "Son without "GOD'S" Permission, "Because we are "Anointed" through "JESUS CHRIST" and the "Holy Spirit". "The three things that I prayed for in my younger years, "I have all "THREE" of them a "SON, my "WIFE" is a "FOREIGNER," I can "SCULPTOR," I can "Build," and I'm a "Journeyman Carpenter," And that was the "THIRD" thing that I prayed for, "And I believe there's more to come, "If you can "BELIEVE" it, you can "ACHIEVE" it, "And if you can see it, you can Build it, give "GOD" some Praise right now,... Hallelujah...... "GOD is good all the time,.. "Come on, "You gotta say that's more than just a "Coincidence, "God, "And the love of GOD, "Is real… "PEOPLE"! I can't EXPRESS this "Enough" …. "That people NEED to just let Go, and let "GOD `,"Talk to Him, "And Develop a Personal Relationship with Him. "And when you develop your personal relationship with "God," He hears you better when you're praying to Him. "And you see with the Personal Relationships, "GOD will allow you to do things that he wouldn't allow me to do, because you went to him in prayer, and I didn't..... Growing up, (I don't know how it was with you guys,... "But with me, "I was always asking the questions, "WHY," "WHY" this, and "WHY" that…Why, Why, Why... "I can remember, My "Mom and my Brother "David," And friends, "Would always tell me, " You should be a "lawyer, "You are always asking "Questions!! ….,"And Why do I talk so much" Mannnnn!!!!!! Why, Why," And what "IF"...."And usually there answers weren't good enough for "ME" anyway, "And I would dig deeper into the story, of whatever they would be tell me at the time, "You see now, those are the things that makes me till myself, (Hmmmmm) "What was life trying to tell me early! (Hmmmmm), I had my warning, I realize now, as I Ponder back on my life, I see what (life) was trying to tell me now, "So young people, "You kind of need to police yourself," And try to know thyself, "Beware of yourself, "But in all, "Be true to thyself," learn to "Motivate "Yourself, "Because sometimes you gotta be your own best "Cheerleader, "And there will be times you will need that little "Extra Bump," "To urge you on, If you can't get it from no one else, "You feel me." So what I'm saying young people, "learn yourself, "Analyze yourself, "Know your "likes, "Know your wants, "Try and see yourself in different ways; "I mean it's almost like you have to go out of your "Body" to look "Back at your "Body, "And try and see yourself for what your "Worth" "Because sometimes, "It can Be, "Just as plain, "As the "Nose, on your "Face" right in plain "SIGHT"... "You just have to realize "IT `... "AND HARNESS IT"... "Then look in the mirror and tell yourself, "I! `SEE! `YOU!... "And I'm "NOT" talking about the reflection of you," I'm talking about inner "YOU"... "When you say; `I `SEE `YOU... "I'm talking about you're "WORTH" your `TOTAL` `EXISTENCE` Who You `ARE` as a `HUMAN` with all of your `BEING` when you are `GLOWING` and `RADIANT` and "Brilliant" to `SEE`, that's when everyone looks at you, "When you walk into a crowded room, `Your very presence, "DEMANDS" "ATTENTION"... "Everyone stops to look upon you, `The `Whispers` In the Crowd are saying, "I have to meet this person, "Whoever he or she is, "Just by the way you carry yourself, "This is where the words, "I "SEE "YOU," Come into "Play. ("I "SEE "YOU") Your, "ENERGY," your "AURA ` your "PRESENCE GLOWS" like an "ANGEL'S Halo ```"" I`SEE"YOU`!!! "One thing I've learned in life, "You're only as good as you "Feel…"So feel good about "Yourself".. "love Yourself" "Respect Yourself," "Because" ``If you `Don't nobody else "Will" "So, "I Don't ask for "RESPECT" I "DEMAND" "RESPECT" and I'll let my "DEMEANOR" speak for "ITSELF"… "And just like I "Demand "Respect, "So shall I give "RESPECT" `But it's the way I walk into a Crowded room with my "Head "Held "High, "And my "Chest Out, "And walking for Sure of Yourself, "With no Doubt, "People will see you when you walk in,…"So walk with" Purpose! "Every "Movement! "Bing for sure of Yourself" (GLYCERIN) like a "(DIAMOND)" out of the "Rough" "You will "EMERGE" "And giving no `Doubt` about "Yourself, "To all those who are watching you, "Most of them, Are unsure of themselves anyway, "Second guessing `Themselves` to "your" very `Presence` "And by now, "Everybody's at your `BECKON` Call(Hmmmmmmmm.) "Have you ever come into a crowded room, "And everybody stopped and started whispering to one another, "And as you walk by, `The looks that you're getting,… ``From half of the room, "You get flirting eyes, "And the other half` Is wondering who `ARE YOU` …"Who just entered the room." They feel as if they haft to Introduce themselves to you. "They want to be a part of `WHATEVER` you have going on, "And don't even know the flavor of your Kool-Aid, "Because they just want to be in your company, "Because of the "AURA" that you're "RELEASING"… "Now this is one gift from God" that you have to be Very Careful with, "Because people will `Trust` You, "And Follow You` "And we'll listen to you, "So many men have misused this Gift, of "Trust," And people were `HURT,` "Yes, some people has even died, "That's how powerful this Gift can be, "People will even lay down their life for you, "For your `CAUSE`, If it is `Strong Enough` If YOU are "STRONG ENOUGH." People Be Aware, "And be `Mindful` of the `Gifts` that "God" gives you; "So don't `Misuse` or `Hurt` no one with your "GIFTS` …"Because they are

"POWERFUL "GIFTS, `So be very careful in playing with people's lives (I SEE YOU)."When I was younger living in "Bermuda, `I used to go down to the ocean to "FISH" although I was a beginner In fishing, "Being a foreigner to the Island, `I had to learn on my "OWN, `But `Three` things I've learned from Fishing, "That I use in life today, "One,…I learned how to "FISH," "Second is, "Everyday can be a Fishing day, "But Every Day can't be a "CATCHING" Day" and "THIRDLY" ("PATIENTS"… "PATIENCE is "Definitely a "VIRTUE" `Yes learning to 'FISH" was Definitely a game changer for me, "For so many different reasons, "Because I apply it to my life; "Guess you say how is `FISHING` going to help me in my life, "Well I'm glad you ask that "Question` "I come to the word `PATIENT'S` again, "I can't Stress this word enough to you, "PATIENTS" will hold you, "It will ease your mind… PATIENTS will keep you from getting over "STRESSED OUT"…(INTEGRITY) is another Virtue, that needs to be treated with "Respect` and probably should be learned in your younger days, "So in your old days, People will trust you by your `WORD`, "Because you would have shown numerous "Examples` (Such As) picking up a piece of paper, "And putting it in the trash, `When `there's no one looking at you; "No one to say to you good job, or to say Awww, You didn't have to do that, "And a person that follows through on their promises, "That's what builds "INTEGRITY" and not complaining all the time about the task at hand, "And expecting nothing from it, "That Person, is truly, a Person of "DEEP "INTEGRITY" you really don't have to tell him anything,`He already knows, "That's why I say people, `Be who you are, `Who "God" made you to be, "No more, "No less, "Shakespeare quotes"…"To Thine Self Be True" End quotes. No one can see you "AS GREAT " IF you don't see yourself, "AS GREAT"; And I'll say to you, "As you try your Greatness, `You still have to be who you are, "And no one else, "The great, "LES BROWN" said, "You ain't got to be "GREAT" to get "Started" "But you gotta get "Started" to be "GREAT" people are going to judge you, `Buy everything you do and say, `So when you say something, "And put it out there, "Make sure it's "Right"... "Because even your "CLOSEST FRIENDS" will be listening to you, "JUDGING YOU" "Watching to see if you're a `Man` of your `Word` and you always want to be a `Man of your `Word`it "SOLIDIFIES" you, `Shows your `Character`; What type person you are, `Your very Essence of a person. "Because people will start to trust you,` And following you, `So you going to warner `HANDLE` that with care," Because once you drop the ball on it, "It's hard to pick it back up, "To win their trust again, "So always be true to "Thyself" ... "And to thy "Word, "It'll Radiate from you, "So that it becomes "INFECTIOUS,".... `And never hate your Enemy`... "Those who are Against You" Because it affects your "Judgment" that will result in making wrong `Decisions` "And that's what you don't want to do, `Is to start making wrong `Decisions` in your life, "And other lives as well." Because think about it, "If I'm mad at you, "I'm very angry. "What happens now? RAGE, ANGER is Building up, your EMOTIONS come into play, "And now it doesn't matter to you, if you go left or right, `Because your `Angry, "And now, "Your only move, is only going to `Satisfy` `Yourself ..."So what's your next move now"..."But is it the right move, "that your trying to make," Would you have done it, or said it, "If you wasn't `Angry` (Hmmmmm), `So now you start to Second-guess yourself, `Whether you should have said it, or done it, (Why) out of `ANGER ` But, was it the right thing to do," The right thing to say to the person, "Making decisions when you're ANGRY with someone is never good, "Because you're not being fair to "Yourself or to the "Person, "Especially to yourself ."And for whatever reason, "Never lose your "ENTHUSIASM," because once you lose your "ENTHUSIASM," you lose your "INTEGRITY" and once you lose your "INTEGRITY," you're a common man. "And who wants to be common......? So learn to control your "Emotions, "Because it can stress you out at times, "And you don't need any added stress, "That's why now, "In my Older Days" I try to "Analyze" every "Situation" In my head "BEFORE" it Happens... "That Discerning Spirit is guiding me, "To see If it has merits for me to even waste my breath on a "Frivolous "Conversation, "That would amount to nothing anyway,...or nothing of Concerns, "So don't waste time with it, "Nor your breath, "Save it, "For important things because, "Who knows when you need an extra breath, or "Two, (Hmmmmm),.. "I like things that make me go (Hmmmmm), "Because; "It makes me "STOP `` and "THINK `` just don't throw things off lightly`, "Because it "MIGHT" have some "MERITS" ……. "Let's talk about the word("FAITH")... "YOU SEE" ``The very reason that JESUS called Peter to walk on water, "Was to show the "SIGNIFICANCE" of "FAITH" …"You can walk on water; `With Faith`..."But keep in mind, "YOU" Better be focusing on two things, and the "First Better Be "JESUS CHRIST"...And the Second you should be screaming "FAITH" don't" FAIL ``me" NOW ``,"AND!!! (DON'T) `look down at your `FEET` "Because soon as you "DO" take your mind is off `JESUS` and then `START` to "DISBELIEVE" as "PETER `DID `..."Because,.." IF you "DO "I got news for "YOU";...."YOU'RE GOING TO SINK" …,"EVERY TIME"...That's how Peter sunk, "When he looked down at his feet, `He was so "Amazed! "To the point that his Faith Failed Him; `Because he took his Attention off "JESUS;... "You see JESUS is the prize, "The main "Gold of …. "JESUS" walking on water; "Not because he could; "BUT" to teach "Peter and the "Disciples to keep their "ATTENTION" on him, "NOT" the "STORM" and not the "CRISIS" at hand, not the "BILL COLLECTOR,"not the "DOCTOR" but "JESUS CHRIST"...`Now JESUS didn't sinked into the "OCEAN" like Peter did. (Hmmmmm)... "So keep your head up, and focused on "JESUS" and don't get Distracted when it comes to your Prayers and your (FAITH). "Because the devil is out to STEAL them from you, "Faith is "Believing in what you "Hope For" "And the "SURETY" `Of what you don't `SEE` ..The devil doesn't want you to `Dream` "Because when you start to "Dream" you start to build "FAITH".... Now you got The devil "SCREAMING"... "YOU'RE KILLING ME!!!.... "SON of MAN,"LOL..., "You see Dreaming is another Mechanism for Building

"FAITH, (Hmmmmm)," let me explain, "Because when you start to "DREAM," you start to see things that you "WON'T, or "WON'T to do in life, "So Now," You start Imagining things, "And Wonder," If I could do those things, or "If I could have those things, "And if you start to believe that you "CAN," "You start to have "FAITH,".... "Do You see where I'm going with this"... "The only way to BELIEVE, "Is to have "FAITH," "And if you have "FAITH" you Definitely Believe, "THAT ALL THINGS ARE POSSIBLE"... "TO whom believes in the "POWER" of "JESUS CHRIST," "That's why the devil doesn't want you to "DREAMS," `I'm sure you heard the quote`, "Only GOD'S Children Dreams" The word of "GOD" says in, Acts 2:17... "In the last days," I will pour out my spirit on all people; and your Sons and Daughters will Prophesy, your Young Men will see Vision, your old men will Dream Dreams. "See the devil," He wants you to have "NIGHTMARES," and Nightmare of Destruction, dreams of lusting, dreams of failure, and visions of killings, and stuff like that, He doesn't want he doesn't want you to see nothing positive, "Nothing what "GOD" has planned for you, "He tries to "Poison The "Minds of all the "Young, and the "Weary.... "You can't let devil beat you out your "DREAMS." The devil want's "MURDER, and "DECEPTION in your "HEAD,... "And he wants you to "HATE your "BROTHER, It's funny how the devil can put a thought or lie in someone's head about his family member, or a friend," And have them against each other for "Nothing, "DON'T!!! Let the devil trick you" And you end up losing that "Family Member," or that Friend, "The devil is a "LIAR"....(Hmmmmm, the word of "GOD," "Says we must put on the whole suit of "Armor ," "That we may protect ourselves, "From "Spirits and "Principalities in High Places. "Another reason why the devil doesn't want you to dream, Is because he knows that "GOD" is the one who gives you "Visions and "Dreams, "And if the he can come in between you and your "Visions, he can come in between your "Dreams and, Connection with GOD; "And not necessarily in that order; "And then he'll starts to knock at your "FAITH, "Wanting to tear it down,

They say there are (Seven) Characteristics to "FAITH,... 1) "FAITH is ``GRACE``, A "SUPERNATURAL" Gift of Standing. 2) "FAITH is not Opposed to `Science`. 3) "FAITH is Necessary for Overcoming Difficult Times. 4) "Grace "Enables "FAITH. 5) "FAITH is the "Beginning of "Eternal "Life. 6) It is " Certain. 7)A human act; "So protect yourself and stay prayed up ,"Because the evil one, "Is out to still "Dreams and "Vision … "By Any Means Necessary! "I've learned to use the devil for my "Purposes Thou, ("Hmmmmm,) (What Do You Mean By "That,) "I'm glad you asked that question," "Have you ever been in prayer, "And while saying your prayers you fall asleep, or "listening to the word! And you fall asleep in the middle of the message, "And you doze off, "That's the devil, "Trying to "Steal the Word of "GOD out of your "Mouth, and out of Your Dreams and Vision, … ."Trying to "Steal your "Knowledge, "Trying to knock your "Faith, Trying to take your "Closest "Memory, "When you're Speaking to "GOD, or "In prayer, "And If the devil can take that from you, "What's in your heart, "from the "Message, or "What you read, "He can try to control your "Faith,... "And how I use him sometimes at night, "It's like this,..."Because" Of my "Sleeping "Disorder, "I meditate some time as well, "But this is the kicker," As long as I think about something "Positive, or on a Massage, I'll fall asleep, "That's the devil's way of trying to steal my Thoughts, and "Dream, and "Visions positive thoughts, "So, "When I'm really tired, "And want to go to sleep fast, "I start thinking "Positive "Thoughts on "Purpose…, he thinks he's stealing, "But he's putting me to Sleep, lol," Because by that time, I'm sleep, "Jokes on him, "Because I'm thinking positive," And he doesn't want that, "So he puts me to "SLEEP," "That's how I use "HIM"(wax on, wax off) "IF I can remember "ONE" Thing In The Morning, "I've "WON," "That's why we must tread lightly, when talking with "God, "Because devil is right there listening all the time," Wanting to put a thorn in your side, or "Just stop your "Mission or your "Dream, `That's why I say, `We must learn to take `Control over our "Dreams" also: "Because, you know you sin "CONSCIOUSLY" as well as

"UNCONSCIOUSLY" and "UNCONSCIOUSLY" is `IN` your "DREAMS" you say, "How do I CONTROL my "DREAMS," "I can't do that!!!,... "YOU CAN DO IT," `let me PROVE it to you, "Have you ever had a nightmare and something or one is chasing you, "And just before you're caught, "you wake up," who woke you up, "YOU DID!! "You woke yourself up, "Because you were ``Scared, "So that means you can "CONTROLLED" your "Dream, "So the next time you're having a "Dream about "Fornicating, "Make believe someone chasing you" and "Wake Up" You can do it, "like you always do, "The more you Practice waking yourself up,"The more you learn to "Control the Dreams"(That Is Starting, and Stopping "ONLY) "Just like you were Scared and Woke Yourself Up, You can Wake Yourself Up when your Dreaming about things you Shouldn't be Dreaming of, "That's why the Bible says, "We sin "CONSCIOUSLY" and "UNCONSCIOUSLY"; well, the UNCONSCIOUSLY is in your "SLEEP": "When you allow your Dream to go on and knowing you can stop it, "But We just "Don't want to Awaken Ourselves, "So you start to sin "Unconsciously. "Faith, doesn't make it easy, "It makes it "Possible... "Possible for you to endure the ``TEMPTATIONS! that you're going through... "Even in your ``UNCONSCIOUS World``, When you're sleeping, And you're somewhere, "Where you're not Supposed Be, in your Dreams, or With someone you're not supposed to be with in your "Dreams,... "So you ask me, how do 1 "Control" this "Situation" or the "Dream" I'm glad you asked me that question, "SIMPLE" ...(WAKE UP,)...Allow me to Re-enervate," Let's say you were having a nightmare, "Someone is chasing you, and just before he reach out to grab you, what do you usually do, "YOU WAKE UP!!!or you are falling off a cliff and just before you hit the bottom what do you do, "YOU WAKE UP!!! or a robber is robbing you and decides to shoot you, and just before he shoots you, what do you do, "YOU WAKE UP!!!or you and your friend are fighting, ``And he pulls out a ``Knife, "And just before he `STABS! you!... "WHAT! do you do, "YOU WAKE UP!!!you see the pattern here, `You had the power to wake up each time you were in trouble,

`This works both ways you know, "You just have to use it, `So when you're somewhere where you're not supposed to be, or Doing things you're not supposed be doing, `While you're dreaming, "UNCONSCIOUSLY" in your dreams, `You have the ability to do "WHAT!... "TO WAKE UP!!, "So dreams are "Controllable," ``If that's what you're trying to do, "You can also Sin Unconsciously while you are awake by not `KNOWING` the `Sin`, "This is why "REPENTANCE" is a daily and nightly thing, "Well it should be in your life anyway, "Faith is believing that it can happen, "So let your Faith be bigger than your "FEET, "That it may hold you up along your walk, "And your journey, "Because you half to have" Faith" be "Great!, "To want to get up, "And go get it.... "JUSTICE," "MERCY" and "GRACE," "Justice" is when you get what you deserve, "Mercy" "Is when someone has compassion on you, "Grace" Is what you get when you don't deserve it. "Faith is a tool for "Christian people, to hold onto in tough times, "Faith is an Important Element to all human life on earth. "Faith is what helps us get through tough times, "lighting up the pathway in times of darkness, "Helping to give us strength in times of weakness. "Faith is a connecting Power into the Spiritual Realm, "Which links us with "God, and makes him become a Tangible Reality, "To the Sense Perceptions of a Person, for we walk by "Faith, "Not by Sight. "But when you ask, "You must ask and believe, "And not "DOUBT! "Because once you "DOUBT ``,"You're like a wave in the sea, "Blowing and Tossed by the Wind. "Because the testing of your Faith produces "Perseverance. "I know it can be difficult talking about "Faith during Hard Times. "And it is certainly tough trusting in the word, "When every single thing in your life seems to be "CHALLENGING" you, or JUST "PAINFULLY AWFUL". "But these bad times" are when Faith is most Important, "Because it can be a life "Raft" in your "Storm" "Faith can always be restored if we're willing to seek it out, "Hebrews 11:1 tells us that, "Faith is the "ASSURANCE" of things "HOPE" for, and the CONVICTION of things "NOT SEEN." Through FAITH, we've been able to keep our heads above the water, "Not because of anything we've done on our own, "But because of the "Faith through "Christ "Jesus, "We are able, :Jesus said in John 8:24 Unless you believe that I am, "Who I claim to be," You will die in your sins. "So people we must believe, And keep your "Faith strong in "Jesus, "You can walk on water, "Just don't look down at your feet, like Peter did… "Don't take your "EYES off "JESUS. "When Jesus was walking on the water, "He called out to Peter, "For him to walk to him, "And he did, "Peter walked on water until he was frightened, "And looked down at his feet, "And all hell broke loose, "First of all he, "Broke his "Faith, "By taking his "Eyes off of "JESUS" And he sinked, "And the moral of that Bible verse, "Was to keep your attention on "JESUS," "So your "Faith won't fail you In time of need, "There are Three kinds of "Faith, "Did you know that?; "I didn't know that, "Until I Research it, `And the three "KINDS" of "Faith, `Are … :#1) Dead Faith;) "The Bible says "Faith without works is dead, "Dead Faith, Exchanges words with action; it's like a body without a spirit. #2) "There is a, ("Demonic Faith") Which means, "Demons also have "Faith they Tremble. It's not Dead "Faith, " but Intellectual and Emotional. #3) "And there is an (Active Faith) It's real and alive. "Faith that's alive is based on God's word, "And involves the "Whole Person "Mind, "Heart, and "Will. "Jesus said if you have "Faith, "As small as a Mustard Seed, you can do "WONDERS. "If you know "God, "Because "God is "Faith and "Hope…"I said earlier in the book, "That you can walk on water," with Faith…"just don't look down at your feet "You see that's what Paul did, "And he lost his "Faith, `Instead of keeping his "Mind and "Attention on "JESUS,… "He looked down at his feet, The Bible said, "And then he began to sink, "Because he lost his "Faith, and took his "Eyes," Mind, off "JESUS," That's why your "Faith has to be strong as you can get it! "How strong is your Faith?" Are you keeping your Mind and your Eyes always on "JESUS," The High Calling, The "PRIZE,"(Hmmmmm), "The Lord, is good to those who's "Hope, is in Him, To the one who seeks "Him "Early, "It is good to wait quietly, "For the Salvation of the "Lord" be still before the "Lord, "And wait patiently before Him, And do not "Fret!!...."When other people succeed in carrying out their wicked schemes, "Because the Lord will give you in due time, "But you have to "Remember, "His Time, Is not your Time, His ways, Are not your ways, "But ``He "CAN MAKE A WAY," OUT OF NO WAY," Trust Me, `You might ask, How can one have Faith, In time of need… "Faith in JESUS, (Hmmmmm), I'm glad you asked that question, "Well, (1) "When you're praying ,Pray for JESUS, and His "Goodness and "Mercy, "You must also ask him to strengthen your Faith…(2) "Doing quiet times, "You need read devotionals, "Study your Bible, "Pray; `Write in your journal, or whatever makes you feel close to ``JESUS, "If you want to walk by "Faith! "You need to release Your Fears to God, `And accept the path that he sends you down. "I know you might say this is easier said than done, "Truly I understand, "Because truly this is a hard task to do, "Even I have not become completely fearless, "But I'm on my way to completing that particular part of my life, "In becoming fearless, "Being able to Speak; `And Act Freely," `Without "Embarrassment, "That's what I'm trying to accomplish now in my life, "Because I have something to "SAY, "And I believe "God wants me to talk for "Him, "SO, "I will, Exercise my "Faith and wait on "God,… It may be hard, And it may seem as if nothing is happening at time's. "I know how you feel, "BUT these are the times of your TEST with "God, "Where Patience is a Virtue, "Where Pressure is applied, And you know what they say about Pressure, it is a known fact that Pressure makes "DIAMONDS," "So we must wait upon the Lord, "And he will bless and "EXALT" you in due time, "So I must learn to draw my "Strength from "God, And not from my own "Self"… "Because it won't work, "My Reliance has to be in "JESUS, "And not take matters into my own hands. "Focus on no one but "God, "And not the "Doctors "Reports, or the "Dow Jones, "If we want to walk by "Faith we need to "Release our "Fears to "God and "Accept the path he leads us down, "This is easier "Said, "Than Done, of Course, "You may not be able to become completely "Fearless, "But you can be Courageous and submit to the will of "God by opening your

"Bible Daily, read, Study, Daily Devotion, "Pray without Ceasing "1: Thessalonians 5:17, fellowship with other Christians, "Be humble, "Serve others, "Confess your Sins and "Repent daily, and "Love others, "Another way to build "Strong "Faith is to, "Memorize and Practice Scriptures, "Reading, and talk to "God Everywhere, "And willing to trust him in your heart, "And most of all, "Build a "PERSONAL "RELATIONSHIP with "HIM, "You see If you have a "PERSONAL "RELATIONSHIP with Him,....When It's Personal between you and "GOD;... "let me explain a little something first, "You see When it's "Personal" "God will allow you to do something, "That he won't allow me to do," When it's PERSONAL, "You have a "FAVOR" You went to HIM in prayer for something or to do something and I didn't, "But you did, "And I were punished and you wasn't, "Did you say "WHY"... I'm glad you asked that question... "Let me give you the Best Example I can in (LAYMAN'S TERMS:) And From the Bible, "The Bible says that "David" was the "APPLE" in "God's eye, "It says, "David sang for God, "And he Dance for "God and "God love him, "Now here's my "Example, "The "TEN "COMMANDMENT" was written before David came about, "And one of them I believe says ...Thou shalt not KILL," "RIGHT," "But! "THAT'S "WAS "ALL "David" did for "God" was "KILL," "I say to you" HE WAS GOD'S "HIRED" "ASSASSIN," "He would send "David on Missions of Destruction, "These are not "MY "Words," "But words of GOD from the "Bible," 1st Samuel 15:3 says "Go and attack the Amalekites! Destroy them, and take their possessions. "Don't have any `Pity. "Kill their "Men, "Women, and "Children, "And Even Their "Babies. "The word of "God,""Said" in, "Numbers 31:17, "Therefore kill all that are of the "Male "Sex, "Even of the "Children: "And put to "Death the "Woman, that had "Carnally known "Men: (End Quotes) "Now that's not "Me Talking" "That's the word of "God," "And why do you think "God had those people "Killed..., "SIMPLY" "Because they were "SINNERS," "And not with "God".... "You see back then that's the way "God dealt with the Sinners. "The Bible says, "David prayed before every "Battle, "So he already knew the "Outcome," And he would begin his battles, "Full Steam Ahead,.. "You know it's something when "God's got your back, "And fighting your battles, "Because first of all, "Your fighting "BEHIND `` "GOD," "And he's cleared the way for you already, "You get to keep all the "GOODS".... ,"The word says, "GOD said go in, "And take all "Possessions" ,"The word say "David took everything that wasn't nail down, "And I would have done the same thing, "With "God on my "Side, "And he give me "PERMISSION"!!!, "You see "God had "FAVOR" with "David, And you already know with "God, "FAVOR" ain't "FAIR," "And "God had all "FAVOR ``for ``David. "So the Moral of the Story is," You must go to God in prayer with everything," And he will direct your path…,"And bless your way; "Take your problems to "God ``"Even the "littlest, to the "Biggest ``.... "Talk with Him daily, "Walk with Him daily, "Be like a friend, "let Him Whisper in your ear, "And you to his, "Develop your "Personal "Relationship with "Him, "So he will allow you, when he won't allow "Others, "Because you prayed about it, "Like "David "Did, "You see, "When you pray about it, And "God Approves of it, "It doesn't matter what anyone else says, "Because "FAVOR" ain't fair when "God's Involved. "He's going to pave the way for you, "So there's no "Obstacles in your way". "He's gonna fight whatever battle needs to be fought for you, "Whether it be "Spiritually" "Physically" or "Mentally"... "God's got your back! "You see, "When you have a "Personal "Relationship with "God"… "It's just like having a "Personal "Relationship, with "Your "Earthly "Dad, with your "Mother or your "Friend, (`they`) will allow you, "To do things that they won't allow others to do,... or "When your Earthly Dad has two children, and "Favor one over the "Other, "And sometimes that happens, "Maybe one is older than the other," And with that, He gives Favor to "One, "He allow him to get away with more than the other, "And it happens sometimes, Some may call it "Favoritism" "THAT'S" WHAT YOU WANT WITH GOD!!! ("FAVORITISM") this is why I can't stress enough, "Too get your own "Personal "Relationship with your "Father" who is in "Heaven"... "That he may show you some

"Favoritism," "So how does one receive "Favoritism" from the "Father" in "Heaven"... "By" "Obeying" "Him" "Like you would do your"Earthly" "Father," "And praying to him daily,..."The word says... "David" `Sang` and `Danced" for "God ``"And he won his heart over, "God" said, " I am a Jealous God!!! Exodus:20:5–6 "So Basically he likes to be Praised, "And talk to Daily, "And Nightly, "The `WORD` says, "David was after "God's own "heart, "He was the Apple, in "God's eye... "It says, he sang praises to "God, "And he dance for "God, "So whatever Praise you need to Praise, "Whatever Dance you need to Dance,"To receive "Favor" or "Favoritism" that ain't "Fair ..."You" need to "START" making it happen, "That you may receive some "Favoritism" or "Favor" that ain't "Fair" ...," But in any case, "You must Believe and have "Faith, "That he can do this, "My Bredrin," "The life of a Christian is not always going to be great, "Because you're going to run into "Difficulties," "And have "Consequences," from the "Decisions you have to make," And sometimes your going to make some "Mistakes, "As a matter of fact, "A lot of your "Problems will start when you become a "Christian, "Because now the testing of your "Faith Begins," "As it did with "Peter" that's why JESUS call to him, "Peter, "Come, `Walk from the boat to me, "Peter was so amazed and excited that he called his name, "To the point that he jumped up out of the boat, and "STARTED" to "WALK" to "JESUS" ....,"Can you imagine what Peter was thinking,.... "STOP".... ``I mean Stop, "And just think about that for a minute,... Wrap your head around that for a while, ``And just try to grasp what this man was thinking at the time, `To jump out of a completely good floating boat, And walk to JESUS, Who was standing in the middle of the ocean, "And without a Shadow of a Doubt, `This man jumped out the boat with all belief, "And with all intentions to walk to JESUS,...."You couldn't tell Peter at that time he couldn't do it, "He had a made up mind, "So people let me tell you, "When you got a made up mind, "You can do anything, And his mind was made up, his mind and his heart was going to walk to JESUS,... "Now I "DON'T" think he said to his self, "I'm about to walk on water to JESUS, "I think he might have said in his heart in his mind, "I'm about to `WALK` to JESUS,... "BUT not walk ON water to JESUS, until he actually realized that's "EXACTLY" what he was doing, And that's when it hit him, "As he took the "First, Two, or Three, steps,"WOW" "I'M WALKING ON WATER" and in a `Split` `Second`, "Something in his MIND said to him, "This is "IMPOSSIBLE" "HOW" can I be doing this, "He thought to himself, "Knowing the physics of it, and said to himself this" IS "ASTRONOMICAL" "ASTRONOMICALLY" "IMPOSSIBLE," "BUT" with "JESUS" "Everything is "Possible, "And what about the other disciples" "Peter was the only one to respond,... "So when" JESUS called out to Peter, "It was for him to "Encounter, And to show him and the others disciples "GOD'S POWER"... "I can just imagine, ``Peter out there, walking around on water, "And realizes; "WHAT THE HELL HE IS DOING!,...., `Because; now he knows what he's doing is "IMPOSSIBLE" yet he's doing it, `Walking `On `Water,..... "And now, By not "CONCENTRATING" on "JESUS," "So he begins to `SINK`, "And that's the thing right their people, "Taking your "EYES, and your "CONCENTRATION" off JESUS will cause you to fail, "I Can Only Imagine seen "Peter" On the ocean walking around, "And then "REALIZING" what hell he's doing was Impossible," "It's going against all Physics, "And yet he's walking, "So like I said, "He took his eyes off "JESUS" "And he began to "SINK"... "And he yelled out to "JESUS" to "SAVE HIM"...." NOW, "I KNOW, "WE WILL NOT TAKE A STROLL ON THE WATER, "But we stroll through "Difficult "CIRCUMSTANCES , "PREDICAMENTS, and "CRISIS, and "PANDEMIC, that we have to call out to "JESUS" to come and save us, before we Sink into our "Trouble and Trials and Tribulations, "That we go through in life, `NOW! this is the time to keep your focus on the "PRIZE, "Which is "JESUS CHRIST." And "When Peter began to "Sink, "NOW, `he knew not to call out to the disciples, "That were in the boat, "He knew who to call on, "He called out to "JESUS" to save him from "Sinking, "Because he knew "JESUS was the only one "CAPABLE" of doing `So`, "Even though we may begin with good goals, and to do good things, In our lifetime, "In some cases our "Faith may Waiver, and when your "Faith Wavers, "You need to do what "Peter did, "Call out to "JESUS" for help," Because, "He is the only person, "Who can help you is "JESUS you see, "We start out with Good Intentions to make Big Accomplishment, thinking we can Accomplish our Spiritual Goals, "But then the "STORM" Comes, and we take our "Eyes off "JESUS" and we start to "Stumble and "Fall. "DISCOURAGEMENT, "DEPRESSION and "DISILLUSION, and a "Pyramid of "Negative feelings begin to kick in," And sometimes you feel the need to call out for help, "To "OTHERS` "INSTEAD" of calling on "JESUS" "First!!, "And you find out that the "OTHERS" (in the boat) "They could not help you, nor do they have the `Answers` that you're looking for, "And yes our "Brothers and "Sisters in "Christ, "Can HELP you "PRAY," they can "PRAY" for "US," "But "GOD" is the "ONLY "ONE, that has the "ANSWERS; "That `YOU` need,"AND THE ONLY ONE THAT CAN HELP YOU!.

I AM MY BROTHER'S KEEPER

"YES, Sir," We are our "Brother's "Keeper, "For the Lord said in "Genesis 4:.... "So what does it mean," I am My Brother's Keeper," "Does it mean that I'm in charge of him? "That I have to run his life? No, "That's not what it means, "But it does mean to love him, "And to try to give him as much guidance as possible, "Try and teach him the ways of "God," "And the `Values` of `Life`, "And to try and show him the snares in life, "That he `May or `May "Not Encounter, "Whether it be "Spiritually, "Physically, or "Mentally, "We must learn how to guide our "Brothers and "Sisters, and lead "Brother's into "Victory, "AS IRON SHARPENS IRON, "ONE BROTHER SHOULD SHARPEN ANOTHER" giving him the tools he needs to "SUCCEED" in "Life, "But most of all, "PREPARING" him "SPIRITUALLY," "That you may Prepare him, "And get him ready for "God" to use in a Mighty Way," "Because it's like this, `If I can't finish the race , "Well then you "PICK "THE "BATON "UP!!! "AND "FINISH "THE "RACE, "SOMEBODY"....., "ONE" of "US," IF

NOT ALL Of US, need to COMPLETE OUR "GOALS" and "FINISH" the "RACE"....."What "God has "PREPARED" for US, "BUT we can't get there without having "GOD'S" peace and love, and understanding in our hearts and minds, we can't be jealous of one another, and "When we see "ONE ANOTHER" Glowing and Shiny, "Because "GOD has blessed Him, "You shouldn't turn to look the other way, "Like you didn't see it, "Congratulate" your "Brother" on all their "ACCOMPLISHMENTS," whether it be "SMALL" or "GREAT"...., "They Need To Hear It, "Who Knows," "You may say something that will "INSPIRE" them to do "GREATER THINGS," "Because like I said, "IF I can't get "There," "YOU GET THERE" don't close the door for everybody, "And then no one gets there, "So,..."What have we `Accomplished "NOW" as ``FAMILY `` or' 'FRIENDS ``.... "NOTHING," In the sight of "God, "We have only pleased `Man, "What's the "Gold,"..."My Gold is to Please "God," "We all need to help one another, "Feed One, Teach One,...Not Fight One or Hold One Back, from Exceeding in Life, "By killing his or her "Dream" "Like telling them they can't make it, or "They can't do it, "Always give them "Encouragement and "Pushing them "Forward with a "Uplifting "Spirit, "Pushing your "Brother and "Sister along the way, "INSPIRING" them to do "Greater Things," You see sometimes, It's what you say to them, "Sometimes that can, "Spark or "Ignite the Spirit in them, to do "Great Things," or to Change the "WORLD" for the "GOOD" … "Even though our "Friends at work," And "Acquaintance's "May tell us, `What we want to `hear, "It's just not same when it's coming from your ``SIBLING`` "Because, "That's when it really takes effect," let me tell you why, "That's because all your life, "You've grown up with your ``Siblings`` we always tried to prove ourselves to one another all through school, "And all through life, "Whether it be "Sports, "Academics, or just `Life` in General, "We always wanted to come home from school, "And show the next "Certificate" or "Metal" that you have `WON` in "SCHOOL``... "To receive Mom and Dad's approval was "Good, "But not like hearing it from your Brother and

Sister, it was more "Satisfying," So that's why we must continue to Uplift "One Another" to help "One Another" to teach "One Another" to inspire "One Another" … "BEING OUR BROTHER'S KEEPER," not his "STOPPER," "BUT "HIS `"MOTIVATOR,"….MOTIVATING!!! "One Another" `TO Chase Their "Dreams, "Because everybody has a `DREAM," ",But not everybody chase's their `Dreams` "And if you were the "Blessed One" to have Chased their Dreams, "I believe your other Siblings should get together and motivate "YOU" to continue on To Success, "Because like I said, "If I can't get There," "You get There," "By picking up the "BATON," "FINISH THE RACE"!!, "FOR if you "WIN `"YOUR SIBLING WIN."

"Because `NOW` you have the `Ability` to do One or Two things, "You can teach them your way, "AND show them the PATH that `YOU TOOK`, or Show them how to `HONEST` their `GIFTS` and `Dreams`,…"They `Got` to give you the `RESPECT` and `LISTEN` to you,…"Because "Obviously their way didn't work out, "And it may not be because of what they did wrong, `It may be because of what they `Didn't Do`; `And was unable to figure it out, `You may see something they don't see," And be able to help them work it out, "BEING" "My Brother's "Keeper" `So let's not be like `Cain, "Who slew his Brother "Abel, `Because he was "JEALOUS" of him, "How "God blessed "Abel over "Cain. "Because little did he know, "God had blessed his gift as well, "He just favorite "Abel's Gift over "Cain, "That's another reason why "God" has given us two ears to listen, and one mouth to talk, "So that we can listen more than we talk, "So let us pray not to be like `Brother "Cain, "Because `JEALOUSY` can do harm to a family, Can tear a them apart, "And can Cut so Deep, "So Deep, That it's beyond repairing, "Because it can, "And it will, "Have you thinking things that are untrue about one, or all of your siblings, "But I tell you the devil is a liar, The devil will sets you up to believe, "That one of your sibling are against you, or all of them; "And it's `FAR` from the "TRUTH, `"He will have you so confused about your `Brother and `Sister, "We can't let him fool us like that, "So let's get together in All we Do, "And helps "SUPPORT" `One Another`, "BECAUSE" "FAMILY" is everything, "When they are behind you, "And Encouraging you to go further,"And that's what we need form our "Brother's and "Sister's," "ENCOURAGEMENT," yes! "We get it from our `Spouse`, "But the words are really `Captivating` when your Sibling is Congratulating you, "And pushing you forward, "Even pushing us to do "GREATER THINGS" ... "Because we grew up with them, "And watch them do things, "And they watched us, "So yes they're input, is very "IMPORTANT" to your "SUCCESS`...... "DON'T SLEEP ON IT"... "WATER," I would like to talk about water, "And the importance of drinking water daily, "Make no Mistake" "Without It` "You Will` "SURELY DIE" `Because the body needs you to drink water every day, "In order for it to survive," And grow stronger, "And believe it or not, "Your Spiritual growth works in the exact same way, "It's like you have to drink water every day, at least 8 cups a day, or you will deprive your body of water, "And your body starts to get thirsty, "And by the time you answer your body, And start to drink water, `You're really already `Dehydrated` and starting to get weak," Until you've regenerate yourself, "So, `Your Spiritual Growth; "It works in the same way, `let me Explain`, Jesus said I am the way, "John 4:14... "Whosoever drinks of the water, "That I would give him, "Will never thirst again; When you have Engulfed and accepted the Blood of JESUS, you are purified, "BUT" you must continue to Drink his water by studying his Word, To show yourself Approved, "Now If you get too far away from his word," That means you not drinking his water, "And your doing your own thing, "Leaning on your own Understanding," "You start to weaken... "Weaken to the point you need to call out on "JESUS" to save you from dying of `THIRST "SPIRITUALLY, "Because, you have not had your "Spiritual Water" (Yet) "or went to talk to "God" in prayer yet," You see you need to talk to "God" every day, "Be Prayed Up" Reading your Bible every day is like a "DRINK" of "living "WATER, trust me, you're going to need it" Because, "Let me tell you, It's scary out there when you're alone,... "Well"...You won't have to worry about that, "If you Married to "God," Because!, You will already have someone to talk to in those times of need, "And if you're gonna need someone to talk to, "God" is the one, `You'll will want to have that `CONVERSATION` with," Because you will need a shoulder to lean on, "Someone to talk to," And you gonna need "Someone to listen to you talk, "All of your problems" When no one else will, "Because let me tell you," That everybody is not going to listen to your Problems;..."Within my "SIXTY" Years of living," I've found out, You can't tell everything to the body, anyway," Sometimes you gotta take it to ``God"... "He has the ear to listen," When no one else will, or "Care about your `Situation` "And doing time's of weakness," "When you think you can't go on, "And you need that little bit of Encouragement ,"That you can only get from from "GOD" and the "WORD of "GOD" That is why our "Belief, and "Trust, and our "Faith must be strong with "GOD! "So that we don't "Give UP"; In Whatever We're Trying to Accomplish;..."That's like me," Trying to Write this Book"...You see" I CAN'T GIVE UP," "I believe that everybody has a turn back moment... "Whether they should go `Forward` or `Not`... "So I can keep on "Writing, or I can give "Up,"But the thing is this,..."I Haft Keeping In Mind"... "If I give Up," The only Guarantee that I can tell myself, "IS that it will NEVER HAPPEN for me, "THAT'S the ONLY GUARANTEE, THAT YOU GET FROM "QUITTIN'," is that it will NEVER HAPPEN , "Not Under This Sun" "The only way, or Possibility remains that it can happen, "IS if I NEVER GIVE UP".... "NO! MATTER! WHAT! they say..."NO matter if I "DON'T" have a "PhD,"... "And some may tell me, "How can you write a book, 'When you have "Nothing``' 'or " Anything to show for... "HOW" "HOW" I'll tell you "HOW" "BECAUSE I have "FAITH"...and I am a `BELIEVER, a `BELIEVER` in "GOD" and my SELF, "And most of all a `BELIEVER` in "GOD"... "So that gives me the right to go BOLDLY, and LOUDLY, before the World, and Chase my "Dreams`` and "Visions,`` AND "NOW!"I'm ready to stop

"PROCRASTINATING" And start Doing…. "YOU KNOW" "Don't!! "TALK ABOUT IT," "BE ABOUT IT"… `So I always wanted to be an "Established Writer, "And "Author, "So why not start writing "Now,… "If I can reach at least One Person, "Just One Person,"… "Then I'll have done my Job" "And that they may Re-evaluate Themselves," And try to Restore their Minds," Because it is a "TERRIBLE" Thing to Waste" `So Restart your mind, "By Regenerating it, `And start "Trusting! and "Believing! in Yourselves, "Because it's never too late… "So I told myself, `` When I started this Book, "That you are going to finish it! "No Matter What It Takes,"… "So when I started writing about my story, "Once I got to the end of my biography, "I said to myself, "Now" What will I write about, So I started to talk to myself about "Faith" `And what I know about "Faith, "Faith in God" and my Experiences with "Faith, Through Jesus Christ, our Lord and Savior, "And so I did a little research on this and that, "And I just continue to flow, "And the next thing you know, "I'm walking through the door, LOL, "So never give up on your Hopes and Dreams, "Because you will definitely lose out, "And my Brethren, "You are gonna haft to learn, to turn your "Mind Off" sometimes, "And stop thinking so much, "I know that I have to, "Because your "MIND" can be your worst "ENEMY"… "It will make you think at times, "All types of Negativity against your own "Family" and "Friends, "That's where the real "Battle "Ground "IS … "IN YOUR HEAD" that's where the "FIGHT" is,…. "You lay down with it,…"You get up with it,…"You go to work with it, "And nobody knows that it's "Gunfire" and "Missiles" going off in your head, "So it's not where you "live," or your "Surroundings" "And believe it or not my Brother, "It's not really the "Money" and it's not the "Haters, nor your "Enemy, it's not "liars, nor is it the "Unbelievers, that's not the Battleground, "That's not the "Storm"…"Stop wasting your time and "Ammunition" "On what people say about you!!! "Because… "IT IS NOT WHAT THEY SAY ABOUT YOU, "that'll stop you, "BUT ``"IT'S WHAT "YOU SAY!!!… "ABOUT YOU" that's going to "DEFEAT YOU"… `You know, `I've come to realize something, "You have to "Separate who you are" from "what you do" Because people will judge you, `By what you do, "In spite of who you are, "Because what you do, "They can see, "Who you are, "Is within you, "Inside of you, "They can't see that yet, "Unless they get to know you, "And by then," They probably have called you everything bad under the sun... "But a child of God (Hmmmmm) But don't let it get you down, "Because we've all done some things in our lives that we are not proud of, "If I had the chance of doing it differently" `I would do it, "But! It ain't going to happen that way, "So I've got to learn to stop beating myself up, "And, "get it out of my head, "Because like I said before, "That's where the real Battleground is..." In your head" So don't let nobody get to you, "And get under your skin, "Because like I said before, "No one has the ability to stop you, "But "YOU"(if you don't buy into what they are saying about you), "And all of that she say he say stuff, "All they need to do is to get you to believe the Negativity "that they are saying about you, "And once you believe in what they are saying about you, "Then your mind works on you, Especially when you're resting, "It just continues to flow black and forward like a broken album, "Playing out in your head," You're wondering, what are they saying about you,"(or is it true what they are saying about me)"That's why I cannot "Express Enough My "Brethren, "To having control over your Own Mind, Because it's only "YOU" that can DESTROY!! "YOU"... "Don't you let those demons in your head bring you down with the Negative thoughts in your mind ..."Because," Believe me they are going try, And Will "Succeed" If you let them, "Stay prayed up, "So the evil one won't steal our "Dreams and "Visions... "You see I have decided to stand up..." Stand up to life, and those demons, "And that, It's not The End! "Until I give up, THERE! is still HOPE! "So I'm going to "Get Up Every Day," `And I'm gonna get out in the world, "And face it's day Challenges, "I will use the "Pain of my "Past to Push me Through, "To strengthen me each day, "To Remind me of the Time I've Wasted, "Time that can never be "Regained, "But you see my "Spirit tells me that I'm still in the game, "That I can still win the Race"... "You see, "I can't afford not to be me, "I can't afford "NOT to just, wake up and go to work" and get a check "I can't afford "NOT to see, "WHAT MY GREATNESS IS "I've got to put my foot," All the way Down, "And see what I can get out of life, "If I really, really try… "I've been getting knocked down, "But I'll keep getting up until "God" says its time out, I'm Empower myself in the word of "God," So that I don't grow worry, "Nor weak, "When something I feel like quitting, "When I'm tired, "When the devil throws all types of stumbling blocks in my way, "Trying to stop me in what I'm trying to "Accomplish" "So that I `don't `finish `WHAT I've started…. "With my Book, "And yes, "I wonder what to say at times, "But you see, "That's the "Beautiful part about it (God)…. "Will show you what you can do, `You just got to give yourself that `Opportunity` or a Chance to show you that you can do anything under the Sun," When you have "God" and the "Lord" "Jesus" "Christ" involved… "Never would I have thought that I could be a writer, "They Say" "Never "Say "Never, "So don't let the devil steal your "Dreams, your "Visions, `Because those are the most important things in your life, `Is your Dreams and Visions, "Because without them, "I Believe, "We have no Direction, and no Purpose, "And the devil is looking to steal and kill every `Dream` and `Vision` that he can, "Because he knows that he is "INTERFERING," "With your "Faith in "God," "And in what God has intended for you to do in life!! Your Purpose, "Don't! believe them when they tell you… "YOU CAN'T!!! "Don't be bothered when the people say to you, "Who are you!...`To even say something, "Because you are a nobody, "And you don't have the right to "Speak, or to "Teach ``"WHO ARE YOU!? "That's when you say to them, (or the devil), "And Shoot To Them" I AM!!!, a "Child Of God ``,"And one of his "Anointed" And said with TENACITY!!! And "Meaning" and "Conviction," "Because the evil one is trying to stop you from being what "God" made you to be, `Look` "l only pray that Everybody has a Chance to do what they was `BORN` to do, "But, we're not gonna get there, "If we continue to listen to what they say we can't do, "Instead of what "I say, "I CAN DO" (Hmmmmm), "There is "POWER" in the tongue!...”But you can't be "Weak "Minded … "Because," If you don't use your tongue correctly, "You can do harm to yourself, or "You can destroy yourself, "Just by the things that you say, "You can make things "MANIFEST" "And I'm into Manifestation," "Not Defecation," "That is why we must be very careful about holding our tongue, "And letting it go at the right time, "So that you Can Speak good things into "Existence" for a "Manifestation". "But we have to learn to tame our "Tongues``"Because, It can get us into trouble at times,... "Watch your mouth," The Scripture says,... "We will eat the Fruit of our words, "So are you planting "Good Seeds" or "Bad Seeds" Because sooner or later, "You're going to have to "EAT`` that "Fruit`` From That `Tree`... "So, "Make sure you're Planting the right type of Seeds, `LIKE` "I am the `Head` and not the `Tell`... "I Am Above and not Beneath: James: Said in the Scripture, "With our tongue we can Bless our Life or We can Curse our Life "So always be Mindful of what you say about any, and everybody and "ESPECIALLY" "YOURSELF".... "Because you can also hurt someone by the things that you say, "Also being offended by someone is certainly going to happen to you, "So get ready for it, "Because you can't duck them all, "And you can't lean into what everybody is saying about you, "Especially" When they're speaking negativity against you, like, "You can't do that, or "You'll never get to that point in your life, "Give It Up, "you see, "You got to know who's speaking into your ear, "Because everybody doesn't want to see you `Succeed`, or get `Ahead`, "They want you to "CONTINUE" to "THINK" like them, "Be like them…. "The Word Says"...., "We must NOT be conformed to this World:But be ye transformed by the renewing of your mind; Romans 12:2…Meaning. Renewing your mind, "Changing the way you think, To create a better life for yourself, "That Honors "God," You know it's strange and weird the way I'm thinking now, "The way I believe that my mind has been renewed, "Because I see life differently than before, "I see my "WORTH".... "What kind of Human Being I really am, "And the "POWER" that I have over my "LIFE"… "Just by changing the way I think about myself, "The

Renewing Of My Mind… "So I say to myself, " Why did I wait so long, "Waste so much "Time"... "Because you know" "TIME Waits for no MAN! Before you know it!... You look up, "And life has passing you by, "You start to see the Gray Hairs growing in, "Don't"! even start talking about the aches and pains to go with it, "You start to believe in "God" more and more, "your Faith starts to get stronger, lol, you start to Believe you can do Anything under the Sun, "But it's a beautiful thing when you can recognize these traits in your younger days, "So don't waste your time young "MEN" and young "WOMEN," `And another thing you must learn to prepare your `Mind, `Body, and `Spirit for the Unseen Catastrophes," And life-changing moments such as "Relationship "Breakups, "Job Ending, "Death in the family, etc. "It's always something "The devil stays busy, "So be careful, and always look before leap, "Because he's lurking around every corner, "With his feet out, "Trying to trip you up, "And to slow you down, "In whatever you're doing, or trying to Accomplish, "Especially if your "Faith is working for you," Oh he's angry "NOW" "you in trouble" look out because the devil is angry now, and he's about to throw a Monkey Wrench in your Situation, "By having something bad to happen, or something go wrong, "So you can almost Anticipate something to happen, "It goes with territory, "You see, "life is going to send you some curveballs, "Some you would have never thought, could happen to you, "So mind yourself at all times, "And who is in your circle," Because when you develop a Reputation of doing good for Yourself, "You become known for that, "You setting high Personal standards for yourself, "And be the BEST at what you do," You're not competing with no one else, "Just mold yourself into the best person you can be, "And I believe that says a lot about a person, "And you can't tell everybody your "Dreams" and "Visions" "Because, "everybody ain't going to see your "Dream" or Want to see it, "You have to be careful, "Because you have a lot of "Dream" killers in the world, "So be Selective, have Certain "Friends in your life, "Friends that would "Enable you to "GROW" "Count Them On One Hand, (that's all you need)"Have Spiritual Friends" so that you can Grow Spiritually, "And have some "PROFESSIONAL" Friends, So that they can keep your mind thinking on business, "Have some "INTELLECTUALLY" "Friends, "So they can always keep your mind Updated and Wondering, or to make you say, "(Hmmmmmm): "Then you have some Social Friends, "To enjoy the fun things in life, But be careful," Because there is always a "Neighborhood" (Judas), "That's the one that will stab you in the back, "And say false things about you to others, "So always be on the lookout for him, "Because there's one in every bunch. "We must start believing in Ourselves, Romans 4:17, "Said" You must have the "Faith to call forward those things that are not!! "as though they were" (Hmmmmm)? "Meaning" `That I must believe and what I'm praying for, "That it will happen just as I'm saying it, I have to believe it, "Before I ask it, "As though it was already there, "I have to "Believe in what I'm saying to "Myself, `About "Myself, "So, when I tell myself,"I CAN! or "I WILL," I GOT TO BELIEVE IT, "Because if I don't, Nobody else will, "So when I tell myself that, "This is "My Time," "I got to "BELIEVE" It, "Because `Now` I believe I'm going through a Change, "A METAMORPHIC" And I'm not "Afraid nor "Shame to Change Myself, "From the "Old Me" to the "New Me! "A `Better` "Expression of "Myself, "And I'm not gonna allow the "Habits" of my "Past" "To stop me from my "TRANSFORMATION": "A NEW YEAR, "A NEW ME, "I want to "EVOLVE" `And` "Get up off the ground, "And start living like a First-class "CITIZEN"... "See "MYSELF" and my "WORTH"..."To be much more than I give `Myself Credit` `For "BECAUSE NOW I REALIZE"..... "The ONE I'm really "FIGHTING ``"It's not "What `THEY` say about "ME ``"That's going to stop `ME`... "Not my "Friends, "Not my "Family, "Not Social Media, "THE FIGHT" is in my head, "That's where the Fight is, "Every time you get a moment of silence from "Thinking, "Your head goes off with random thoughts," With all types of Negativity Thoughts,` like` "I can't do `THIS` and I can't do `THAT ` We go to bed with these thoughts and We get up with them, "Sometimes you even Dream of them, "That's why now,

"I've learned to keep Positive Thinking, "And positive thoughts at "ALL TIMES" now, "Because all those other `Entities` can't stop me, "It's only "WHAT" "I" say, "About ME!... `THAT` will shut me down, "YES" That's where the real "Battleground" is, "IN YOUR MIND".... "And it will cause all types of "Stress, And "Pressure, " And you know what they say about "PRESSURE"...."That Pressure can boost a Pipe: "A Galvanized Pipe: "So what do you think "Pressure" would do to your Head, "It's the same Pressure: "I'll tell you what It can do to your head, "Bust it wide open, "As if you were Smashing Grapes, "That's why I had to Renew my Mind, "A new way of "Thinking, and Processing my Information, "Because, if you don't have a "New "Mind, "You'll find yourself doing the "Same Things," "OVER and "OVER Again,... "So I've Changed my way of "Thinking, "And I started to have "Dreams and "Visions, "Because" "God said:"That A man without "Dreams" and "Visions, "Shall Perish." He also said in Acts 2:17, "I will pour out "My "Spirit on all People. "Your Young Men will see "Visions, "And your Old Men will Dream "Dreams … "When the last day comes, "I will give my Spirit to "EVERYONE"

 "So now I've learned to wake up in the "Mornings "Expecting Something Positive to happen in my life today, "Because I've been Dreaming "Big" all night long, "And now I'm "Hungry for Success Now! "I Only wish I would've gotten hungry in my earlier days, "Because so much time has been wasted, "But it's not too late," NEVER THAT," "And now my "Dreams have gotten even "BIGGER" "Because I not only have a "SON," "Now I just got my "FIRST GRANDSON!!! Hallelujah!!! "God is "Merciful` "God is Good" All The "TIME," `And with that being said, "I want to leave a legacy, `For my `SON, and `GRANDSON, "And I "Will"... "If I can "JUST" reach `ONE` `Mind`..."JUST ONE".... "And turn it for the "GOOD ``... `WELL THEN`..."I've done my Job, "And if my "SON" and "GRANDSON" `Will` read this book, and `Receive some `WISDOM` and `KNOWLEDGE` from this Book, "MY `FIRST BOOK"... "I will be a very blessed "MAN, "And, "THANKFUL! "And, "HUMBLE! "And I know a lot of people are going to say all types of `Negative Things` about Me, "Because of this book, "Let me tell you some of the `Things` they're `Going to `Say … "Who is He Supposed to Be….. `His`(Father) "Be that as it May, `They are saying` "BUT" `He wasn't in his SON'S life, "At times when he really needed him, "During the second part of his life, "When he really needed a `DAD` "And a shoulder to lean on,… "And they would be `RIGHT`,… "And I am `So "SORRY" for that"… "That I `Missed` A good part of my Son's life as he was growing up,… `And I have to live with that for the rest of my life, "I'm deeply sorry for it, "But, I got to get over it, "And move on, "Because, "God still bless him to be a "Good "MAN" and "A "GODLY" "MAN!… "And I `BELIEVE` it's because "I PRAYED" for him in his "Earlier years of life as a "INFANT" one night, `I took him out one night, "And I held him "UP HIGH," in my two hands, up under `The "Bermuda" Stars`, like `KUNTA KINTE` did his First born, `In the Movie *"ROOTS"*… "I held them High to the Stars, "And Prayed for Him, "For his SUCCESS, And to be a "GODLY MAN" and "God" had Instilled `Into him the life, "That I Prayed for "Him, AS a "Baby, "So that, "If he will only `Believe and have `Faith in the "GOD" `Above, `He will "BE "BLESSED,"…"So when I left the Island, `After my `INCARCERATION``…`I went back to the States, "To "Atlanta, "Georgia. I entered into a dark place in my life, "The whole time I was there, "IT was "DANGEROUSLY" "UNBELIEVABLE," "My "FAITH" was Challenged," Through "ADVERSITIES," and "ATROCITY," "But without `My` "Faith`, `I don't think I would have made it, `NOR, `SERVED` , "IT was only by his "GRACE" and "MERCY" that I survived, `And standing here today, "Able to be a witness for "GOD," `That he can `Change` lives, "If you "Change the way you `THINK` "And develop a "New Mindset"… "If you will only have the "Faith" that a "MUSTARD SEED ``has, `that he spoke about in his `WORD`,… "Listen, "I've come to terms with that, `I can't do it by Myself … "You'll start off with good Intentions, "Thinking we can "Accomplish your `Spiritual Goal.` "But then the STORM COMES,

`And we take our "EYES `` off "Christ `` "We start to "STUMBLE," and "FALL". "DISILLUSION," "DEPRESSION," "DISCOURAGEMENT," a `PYRAMID` of `NEGATIVE` "Feelings begin to kick in. "And then sometimes, `We call on others for help, "Instead of calling on "JESUS" `First`. "Then we find out that "OTHERS" `do not` have the RIGHT" and true "ANSWER ``... `You see, our "Brothers "and "Sisters in "CHRIST `` Can help us "Pray"... "They can Pray for Us"... "But"... "God" is the only one with the "RIGHT ANSWER" that you need: "Hebrews" 11 is the "Faith Chapter," Where "Faith" is Mentioned twenty-five times. (I counted them) "You would think that "Faith ``must be very Important. "Faith" is deeply rooted with the Expectation of Good Things to come. "MOST of the "Hope" that we have, "lives in your mind, "Faith is buried in the "Heart and in the "Spirit. "Faith can't be Explained by "REASON or "LOGIC" or "DIMENSIONS, "It is not a Problem of Addition or Subtraction, "Can't drive a Car without "Faith"…"Faith, "That someone won't cross the "Divider, and "Crash" into `You. "I believe that, "Faith is just as "IMPORTANT" as the "AIR" that you `BREATHE`. "Oxygen in the `AIR` `Nourishes` the `Body` "And "Faith" Nourish the `Heart` and `Soul`... "Faith isn't just a Notion that some people, "Hold onto, ``In tough times, "Faith is an Important Element, "To all "Human "Life, "Life is "PRECIOUS ``"But it can be very "Difficult! at Times, "Faith is what helps us get through it all,... "It lights up the Pathway in Times of DARKNESS," And gives us strength, `In times of "WEAKNESS," "I am "NOTHING `` without" FAITH `` `No matter what the "SITUATION" is, "NO matter how "BAD or "DIRE you think it might seem, "Your "FAITH" can, "And will get you "THROUGH". "You have to ACCEPT that as "FACTS ``,"And hold on to the "EXPECTATION of "GREATER things to "COME ``... "You can't stop SEEKING or SEARCHING for an ANSWER to help resolve whatever SITUATION you might be facing in your life. "I believe now, "If you really want something out of life, "And I mean really, really, "Wanting" something, "Deep" down inside, "And you have a Strong Enough reason that you ABSOLUTELY must ACHIEVE it, "Well, "FAITH" is a VERY thing that helps you see it Through. "It's the very thing a persistent heart would be. "Never give up your Hopes, and Dreams, "Just because you're facing setbacks in life, "Because that's ALL it is a Setback, "A Moment in Time, "But it's not "FOREVER ``..."And not too Late, "We have to learn "ASAP" about keeping our "FAITH" STRONG" And you'll soon come to realize "WHY" having "FAITH" is so important to have in life right now, "You're going to need it, "Things are going to happen to us in our lives, "And people are going to say untrue things about you… "And going to try and make you feel weird, "And out of place, "And not able to go on, "But if you got "FAITH" and you HOLD on to it, "And know what it "MEANS," You'll pull through, "Because YOU have come to "REALIZE" and to NOW, "That no ONE! can stop "ME, "BUT! ME" you see my SON I've learned that now, "IT wasn't my Friends, "It wasn't my Family, "It wasn't the Internet, "It wasn't my Job,"But it was "ME" all the time, "Telling Myself I can't do "This, "And I Won't be able to do That,:…. "You didn't go to College…. "Just shutting Myself down, "Killing all of my "Dreams, `Because`, "It's My finger on the "Trigger, "That's "IN" my head, "No one else can turn your "Dreams and "Visions off, "BUT YOU," "I'm the only `ONE`, "Who can turned the light OFF, "Now"….If you've already turned it off, "YOU'RE" the only "ONE" who has the `Ability` and `Power` to "REACTIVATED" or turn it "BACK ON" And I just paid my "BILL" to "REACTIVATE" my "MIND" to "REACTIVATE" My "INTELLIGENCE" to "REACTIVATE" my Get "UP" and "GO" to "CONTINUE" my "PLIGHT" in "LIFE"… "God" is good all the Time, "Hallelujah" to the most HIGH… "MY "SON" you have token yourself a "WIFE"… `Now let her be SATISFYING to you, "And "Her to "You …"That you guy's need "NO" "ONE" else, "Because TEMPTATION is gonna creep up on you guy's sooner or later, (A JEZEBLE) is what the Bible calls them, "So my "SON: "BEWARE" of a JEZEBEL…There's one Awaiting around Every Corner to try and sub do you," The trippy thing about it is, "They're gonna know you're married" And have a "Child" "Now there's a couple of different ones, `That are going to try to come after you, "And I'm going to Explain to you, `Which `Ones `They `Are, "And how they're going to OPERATE.. OKAY…"There's one, that probably figures that you're all "Stress Out, "And she's been digging you for a while anyway" "But the opportunity never presented itself… "UNTIL NOW" "When she sees you out and about "this" Particular time, "And she says (Hmmmm), "I Wonder, (As She says to herself) Silently walking towards you, "(And then says to herself), A closed Mouth Won't Get Fed".... "Thinking of having you for "SNACK before her "ENTREE, "SMOOTHLY " SHE, looks down at the baby carriage, "And she's going to say "HOW'S the Baby doing, "let me see how Handsome he is, "Now, she's trying to get Closer to you, "Because; "Not yet has she asked you, "How is your "Wife" doing…"Which should have been the First thing she said, "If she was "Genuine" But instead she says, "Here's my number, "In `Case `you `Ever `Need `Someone to `Talk to, or `Need a `Shoulder to `Lean `On, "I'll be there for you,("YEAH "RIGHT) I BET She Will)... "THEN: "You have the ONE or the ONES, "That think they should have been the one, "Instead of your "WIFE," "You have to really watch out for those ones, " They can really start trouble for you, and `SO `Many `Different ways, "And the funny part about it, "They don't even care who they're hurting, "As long as they can hurt you: "You see, `They can't come to reality, "That you've gone Another Way, " They're going to, try and "Entice you at all cost, "Just to see if they can throw you `OFF` your `SQUARE`, "And you mess Up, ("So Don't Fall For It") "WALK AWAY FROM HER!!! "WALK AWAY FROM HER!!! "And then you have the ones, "That will try and give it to you just "BECAUSE" "Just so they can run and tell your "Wife!.... "Watch out for those "SKEEZERS" as well. "Because they will come for you, "Sooner or "later,..."And you know," You're going to be more `Attractive` to them being Married, "Than "UNMARRIED…" Let tell you why, "First of all, "They don't have to Deal with `You, `Hang `Around, "And following,

"All up behind them, "When they are finished with you sexually, "All they want you to Do, "IS JUST GO," "And leave "ALREADY" …"Plus you already know, "IF you," HOLLOW" in the "SOUTH SIDE" `loud Enough` "You'll Hear it on North Shore!, "And if you `Fart in the "East" you're `Smell It the "West," "In other Words".... "The news is going to `Beat` you "Home"... "So be careful `My"SON`"There is Always" "Someone Watching "YOU" … "Especially in Bermuda"

FRIENDS

"How many people have them, "let's be Friends" The ones you can depend on, "Friends" The Bible says, "There's one that "WILL" stick closer than a "BROTHER": `Choose your Friends very wisely "SON".. "like I was saying to you earlier, "About having Certain Friends, "In certain Categories," Be Selective, "You want to have "Friends" `that want something out of life, "And Hungry to Get Ahead, "Just As You are,..."You got to Pull away from the One's, "That's gonna hold you back," Pull away from those One's, "Who doesn't have a `Vision` or your `Dream` "You got to Pull away from those "ONE'S! "As `Far `As `You `Can..... "Let me tell you another way of "Selecting "Friends, "If you are the `Person`....`That all your `Friends` "Come to for "ADVICE" all the time, "And for `Their "PROBLEMS"... "That's because, `They see something in you, "But you got to remember this thou, "If You're The Smartest Person In Your Group" "Well then, "How are you going to learn more, "How can you "Excel" or "Transform yourself into a `Better You` "A "Higher "You...... "If you're the one giving All the `INFORMATION` `Out` or "SOLVING" everybody else's "PROBLEMS".... "You Need To Upgrade To A New Group,"... " Putting people in your life that will "MOTIVATE" "You"...... "Help you to `Grow` "MENTALLY"... "Then you need someone in your life to help you to `Grow` "SPIRITUALLY" "And someone to help you to `Grow` "PHYSICALLY"... "It ain't Nothing" " You just got to "Upgrade the "People and "Friends in your "Life, "You "Cannot" be the "GO-TO PERSON" in the group all the time..... "It'll Run you

Down," Just Upgrade `Some` of your "Friends, "Not all of them, "Because some pretty sure a lot of them that I have meant or some pretty intelligence some real stand up guys But you know better than me who is who just be aware `, "And another `Reason` Why` "You'll want to keep your `Social` `Distance` from Certain "Friends, "Who don't want "ANYTHING" and "Nothing out of "Life" "Why"... "Because, `They'll rub off on you, "Social `Distance` Yourself from those `People`... "Who don't want to do "ANYTHING" or "Have "ANYTHING" out of life, "And I know your heart `SON`, "You want to help everyone, "And I know, "I get it," Because "THAT'S" the kind of Person, that you are, "You will Try," Even if they don't want to be helped, "But from what I see "Son, "The friends that you have, `Are a pretty good bunch, "They are some "Stand Up Guys" "Now" `Those` are the ones, "That you'll want to keep on your team, (SHOUT OUT TO THOSE BOY'S) (EYE AND EYE) "But, things change, "And will Change"...... "Since you've gotten "MARRIED," "Some of them "Might Say" "All look at Him`, "He's Changed," ("AS YOU SHOULD") "have," "Because now you're Married Man now, "You can't do the things that you used to do, "Go places you used to go with them, "And some of them may take offense of that, or "Become(JEALOUS) Call it what it "IS" (Hmmmmm), "And then you "BUYING" a "HOUSE," "And have a New "BABY "BOY" "And a "New" "BEAUTIFUL "BLACK QUEEN"... "Right now you're "SHINING" Your lights are "Very Bright" Now, `So, Bright" That there's some people that's going to want to put your lights "Out," "Because of `JEALOUSY` You're star is shining too bright for them,` And these are going to be people in your own Circle, `I'm talking about Family and Friends, "It's going to be such a "FACADE`.... "That it's going to be Impossibly hard to figure out, "Who's "Who, everybody will have a mask on, `So now you have to rely on your "DISCERNING SPIRIT" "Always Pray For A Discerning spirit "SON" that would allow you be able to "DISCERN".... WHO'S Who, within ten minutes of the conversation, "You'll be able to "DISCERN" What kind of Spirit you're talking to,...

"The more you rely on it, "The stronger it gets, "You be able to feel the `AURA` that is `Released` from a person, "Good Aura" or "Bad Aura" "You see, `We all have `Aura` that is Generating from our `Bodies`...... "That's the `Halo` that you see around the top of JESUS head that be `GLOWING`, "So praying for a `Discerning` `Spirit` would be in your best `Interest`, So that you'll be able to `Discern`, "A Good Spirit or Evil Spirit,... "It will show `IT'S` Face to "You," By "DESIGN ORDER" "YES" That is One Trait, `That` you must `PRAY` for "Nightly for, "IT will "Literally" save your life one day, "Meaning, `You'll be in a `Situation` one day, "And it'll tell you to move `Forward, `OR` to move `Backwards, "Just in the nick of time, "Then you wonder, `What` moved you,.. Or, "Man" I moved just in the nick of time (Hmmmmm) "The Discerning spirit".... "And then you have some friends, "That'll talk about you behind your back, "Say all types of untrue things about bought you, `To other people, `In an `Effort` to try to Screw your Name up, "You got some that would even tell your `WIFE` Untrue things about `You to `Her, "To try and ruin what you have, "Because there are `JEALOUS` of your Relationship,...."Miserable" about "Theirs , "They want what you have, "And can't have it, `So stay prayed up, "Tell your Wife to stay prayed up, "Because they will come after Her too, "You both need to Pray for a Discerning Spirit, "Because when they say stuff to "Her" about you, "That's Untrue She needs to be able to `DISCERN` the "Real Truth," "And when they say things about "Her to "You,..`You need to be able to `DISCERN` the real truth, "AND "KEEP "YOUR "BUSINESS "TO "YOU "AND "YOUR "WIFE.... "What happens in your home, "Or What is talked about in your home, "STAYS," "In Your Home"... "And I know you know how to pray, "But Teach your Wife to Pray Also....,``IF"..... `She doesn't `Already` know how to, "Because a Family that Preys Together, Stays Together," `And then Teach your "Son to "Pray, `When it's His time to learn  , "When you take a Lady, `To be your `Wife` you are "GROWING" "MENTALLY," "SPIRITUALLY," and "PHYSICALLY," `And you might have `Friends` that are `Not

Married`, "They are now saying, "That you've CHANGED, `And "YES," You should have "CHANGED,"... "You become a `MAN` "Now, "And put away "Childish "Things ``"And if they are not on that level, "Will then it's time to move on,... "Because, `You` don't want anybody to be like an 'Anchor,' `Holding` you "Back,"....`And `Weighing` you "Down!,...`You might not be `Negative` towards them, "But at the same time you need to be "Conscious" of it,... "And, take care of it; "Another Thing".... "FRIENDS; will start to notice "AND" Take account, Of times you turn them down on offer to hang out, "When you Say` NO" to them, "They be like,.... "Hey man you hanging out with the boys tonight, "Or, "Can I borrow a couple "HUNDRED DOLLARS" "Not Understanding when you say `NO` "It's because you have a, "Family Now" `And anything can come Up, "At any time, "So you need to be ready for your `Family` at All Times, `So if you find yourself with friends, "like this,... "let's say you guys went out for dinner, "The next step is always ``let's go to the Bar, Boys, "And you say "NO…" I got to home now to my Wife, "She needs me …"Now this is how it's was gonna go" You'll say, "Now, I enjoyed having dinner with you guys, "But I'm going home now to my `Wife: "And then they'll say, "What do you mean you're going home, boy?," "Aren't you going to come to the bar with us, "Just for a couple,..." Now, "You don't owe anyone no `Explanations,` `For your"ACTIONS"..... `But you `Kindly` say, "That you have to get home to your "WIFE".... "Now, Some of them are all `Wondering`, "IF" there's something `GOOD` to a Marriage life that could benefit them.. `And then they start questioning themself, "And the "LIFE" that they're living: "ALONE ``.... If they're on the "Ascending Path: or on the "Descending Path: .... `You have the type of Friends, "That are really good `Guys`.... "I believe that they'll see, the `Error, in their ways, "And they'll question themselves, "And they'll look to you, "As an "INSPIRATION" ….., "But If they start degrading you, "And really start tearing you down, "By saying, Oh he's "CHANGED," "We don't like the new Him, "Well then, "You know what you have "Discovered, "That these guys really wasn't your Friends in the begin,..... "Friends Lift, "Friends Up," "Especially when you are trying to go to 'Higher Places' ,... "Here's another thing, "Do not `GOSSIP`, "Because the minute you're not around, "You're probably getting talk about as well, "GOSSIPING" that's one of the most "FEMININE" things that a `MAN` can do, "And one of the worst things, "That a `MAN` can do,..."So you just turn away, "Walk away and don't Engage in Conversations that are Frivolous, "And have no meaning, "Because if you're doing it, I "GUARANTEE" you, "They were talking about you too, "I know that sounds tough, `When you're growing up, "And what's going to happen over time; `They'll gonna to fall away by the sea shore, "It's just like a pair of shoes, "You've outgrown them, "They are all just like a pair of shoes, "They just don't fit no more" And it's gonna be the same thing with some of your Family as well, "Because when you begin to develop, "And roll into new "INTERESTS, `And New "Ways, "Behaviors, and "Character! "Over time it's gonna get simpler for you, "IF It doesn't Fit," "Don't Force It"... "IF it "Doesn't make "SENSE `` it "WON'T make "DOLLARS ``..... "You'll start to attract different, and more people, "That will Resonate with the New "You...." When you're growing up, "You're "CHANGING" and the people around you are "CHANGING! "And as they "Should" "Just by the way you carry yourself, `And the "CONVERSATIONS" that you used to have," You're not having anymore," Now! "You want to talk about "GROWTH" and "DEVELOPMENT" and "DISTRIBUTION"... `And Different "BUSINESS! "ADVENTURES! "Building your "PERSEVERANCE,"..... "DON'T! "WANT! "ANCHORS! "They'll slow you down, `You have to let them "KNOW"... NOW! "That, "There's a "New! "PATH!" that you are taking! .... "SELF-LOVE".... "How much do you Love "Yourself, "Because, `Until` you Understand the Value of "SELF-LOVE," you will never have "Friends, or "People "That will be," Willing, "To follow you, "Most people here, "Are running around "Empty, "No Sense," of `Self`, "I say "SELF-LOVE" is very "Important," " I "Already know Son, "You have a lot of "That," lol,... "But it's nothing to do with looks, "Nothing do with cars, or the Internet, "And any other Superficial things, `That one`, Would assume that could make someone love them, "Love" "Yourself even more, "It's a "Matter of "knowing `Your` `Value`, `Your` "Worth"......"It's a Matter of``YOU`` saying,... "I don't have to be around This "Environment! or "Put Myself, In different and strange "Situations! "In Order for me to finally see the `Value` in "MYSELF".... "I had to see "Myself"... "For... "Who ... "I... "Really "Am,.... "In order, to start `Love` MYSELF" For `Who` I Am, "So, I've learned to "Love Me, "Some Me! "So It doesn't matter, "If `YOU` "Love "ME or not, "Because, "I Believe in "Me! "I know "Myself "Worth! "I, "Now know what I Am Here For! "And I have A `Purpose` in life!...." I WILL!! "GROW" through what I've `Experienced` in life... "Yes, with, "All my" Adversities, "And "Setbacks"... "And "Let Downs"... "And, "NO upon NO'S,...."Has taught me to "CHANGED" my way of thinking,..."So that I can see my `Road Clearly`, "So that I can see my "Dreams" and "Visions" Clearly, "So that I can go to the next level, "But in order for me to get to the next level, "I got to let some people go in my life, "As well, ... "You will, `Have to let go of `Some of the people in your life, "That's going Hinder you, "Or `IMPEDE on your "SUCCESS, Or "Slow you Down," "Or, "Get you in "Trouble,..."Even In your "Marriage Life," "And, From getting you the next "LEVEL"... "One reason being... "They're not thinking like "You" now, "Because you are a Married man; A Family Man; "And "They're "Not," `And that's not a bad thing, "But it's not your thing, "Because, "You're took in a different route in life, You have decided to be a, Married Man! "And have "Responsibilities" "That they don't have, `And it might be a little "Harder" "For "Them" To see the things the way "YOU" see things, "Or seeing them, "At this point in time in your life..... "And that's probably because they're thinking "Double-headedly" `While you are thinking Single-headed (Hmmmmm) (Don't let that go over your head...,Lol) "But, "You have a "Wife Now" and a Child"....."To look After, "To Raise" To help Him see, "And Figure out his "Future!" And a brand new Home to

"Maintain," "So you haven't got the time to hang out with them the way you used to;..."Some of them `May` Get It, "And A `lot` of them `Won't`.... "Those are the ones that you have to walk away from..." That doesn't get it..." Because it could have some serious Implications, "On your "Marriage, and "Your Family"... "And we don't want that,..."YOU"... Don't want that!... "And, `You're going to find out, `As you go through your `Marriage Life`, "That More and More People, "Are going to Love You ... "And More and More People are going to "Hate You, "And most of the time, "For No "Reason At All," ``"They will look for a reason to be Mad at you, or "Hate you, "Just because you and your "Wife were Shining and Glowing like `New` `Money`,... "They or not going to like that so much" They're going to Criticize you, `For Being`, "And" `Doing Good`, "And the most hurting part about it is, "A lot of them are going to be "FAMILY" Members "That's going to hit you where it hurts... "IN YOUR HEART"... "It's going to be hard to believe, that, "Some of the "Things, "That your own People are going to say, "And, `Put you through, "It's going to be "Pure "RIDICULOUSNESS," and "JEALOUSY," "On their Behalf, "No matter `how much` you've help them In the past ,"Even the ones you're in the process of Helping Now! "Will still speak ill of you, behind your Back! "Watch what I'm telling you! "And that's `Sad to Say`... "That's Why," "You "Gotta hand pick your Company Now Days," "Some that won't turn their backs on you in the time of "NEED," "Or "Friends, that want to try to "kill your `Dream; "Because all your `Friends, and `Family` "Don't "Won't to see you "Happy"...  " Or That you got "Married," Or "That you have your "First "Child" already before them...,"Or that you moved into your "New House" "Already".... "So what you need to do is, "Take a look at the `Five` `People` That is in your Circle, "Those People, "Will, `Reflect` "Not Only" "Who You Are," "But what You're, "Going to "BECOME,"...`Because, if you're hanging out, with "SMART" and "INTELLIGENT" people you can't help but to get "SMARTER" and more "INTELLIGENT"....IT'S the law of the land,... "IF you `Lay` down with `Dogs`, You're going to get up with `TICKS` and `FEE'S`... "Your Friends are going to Determine a lot about you, "They're going to be the ones, "That will `Mode` into "Success, "To Excel you in life,... "The reason being, if you in the Right group... 99 percent of the time, `We try to Imitate our Friends, "So if you got Friends, that are trying to do things, And have Businesses and a good "SPIRITUAL" "FAMILY" "LIFE"; `You can't go Wrong`, By trying to Imitate them, or "Out "Do "Them, `It's going to make you seek for more, and won't more... "Now it's become a `Competition` thing to `Excel` in life, "How good is That," It's a "WIN-WIN" "Situation, "But, `If your Friends don't want anything out of life, "YOU'RE not Gonna want anything ..."It's your Friends that's going to Mold and Shape you… "Communication with one another, "IT'LL hold all you Guys "ACCOUNTABLE" to each Other, "And they can help pull you "Back on "Track, "When you get "Off "Track," "That's gonna be Really Important, "And the `KEY` to your Survival, `And "Trusting the Process,".... "For the things to Come," And to "MANIFEST," "Everything is a Process," "Rome Wasn't Built Overnight," But you can't get "Discouraged when its not happening for you, In the time you thought it would happen, "Because, "With "God," "Our Thoughts" or "Not His Thoughts,"... "Our "TIME ``,"IS Not His "TIME ``,"And with "God" Everything Happens, "At the "APPOINTMENT TIME"... "With him, Everything will be done "Decent" and in "Order ``... "You're Anointed Son".... "So, "Being Anointed"... "You have to go through a `Process` "And just because you don't see anything `HAPPENING, "Doesn't mean "God" is not working in your life, "It's just a Matter of Time Before you're `Appointed "Time Shows Up, "To often, "We have the "Anointing; "But we get "Discouraged by the "Process.. "When we're not making "Progress... "You have to remind yourself, "That it's all a "Part of the "PLAN! "Don't run away from the "Process" (like I did) "It Will Work … "It's Called "PATIENCE," "Something"... "I" DIDN'T have in my younger "Days, I was like a blue tail fly, "BING "BING "BING,.. "I was all over the place," But in the right Place, "I've told myself Recently,

" IT'S NOT TOO LATE" that age is nothing but a number, "And minds is "UNLISTED" And "REMEMBER".... "This is "NOT to "DISCOURAGE You," "BUT TO ENCOURAGE YOU" "And to prepare you for your Future Blessing," And for events to come, " Already you've been blessed to Buy a `New House, "And you want to keep your "Blessings "Continuously coming to you, "And by doing that, "This is what I mean, `You can't let people get to you, "And make you `Angry` and cause `Evil Spirits` to come into your mind," And Change the way that you are thinking, "And cause you to lose your "BLESSINGS"...., "Don't allow "Family and "Friends, To, Change your way of "Talking" or "Thinking" "Because when you "Believing in Something to Happen, "Or to work in your life, "Your Spirit is always listening, "To everything you say, "Good Thoughts" "Evil Thoughts".... "Bad thinking can cause you lose out, or `Slows your Blessings down` "You gotta be Mindful of the things that you say, "Or keep in your Heart, "Because it'll slow your blessings down; "The way you think , and feel in your heart, "Is going to "Determine how your "Blessings will come to you, "And how "FREQUENTLY" they will come... "You got to always have "Peace and "Love in your "Heart, and "Forgiveness for "People, "It's all right to get "Angry" "But do not Sin, "Good and Evil can't be in the same place, "At the same time, "They can't Occupy the same space.... "Light can't be in the same place as "Darkness, "Light doesn't "Allow it to "Be... "So, "If you have Evilness in your Heart, "The "GOODNESS," "That's trying to get to you, "Can't" get there, "Because of the Evilness that has Consumed you, "GET IT OUT" of YOU.... "And keep it "OUT! of "YOU! "So that your Blessings will always come to you, "So watch and guard your Attitude, "And the way that you treat people...."Let people say one thing about "Daniel!... "That he's the "SAME WAY ``"Every time You See "HIM`, "He doesn't "CHANGE ``"So don't lose your Blessing by "THINKING" Or "SPEAKING BAD"...., "You have to rule your "Emotions"... "So you won't get TEMPTED to get a `BITTER ` taste in your mouth ABOUT SOMEONE, "At the same time, "Thanking "God" for how he's "Blessed you. "So, "Don't let `JEALOUS` people steal your "BLESSING".... "Don't let people that are never going to be with you or for you, "Keep you from the "Blessing that "God" has for you, "Just let them `Do the talking, "You don't have time to "Deal with, "Every "Negative "Comment and "Thoughts that "People or "Peoples may have, or may not have said about you, "And "Especially" the "INTERNET,".... "When you stop giving the "NEGATIVE TALKING" your time, "And "ATTENTION" to things that you've "HEARD," or `By What Someone "TOLD" You....."The better off you're going to be,... "The Word of "God says... " Genesis 3: 8-11, says: "Then Adam and Eve heard the sound of the Lord God as he was walking in the garden in the cool of the day, and they hid from the Lord God among the trees of the garden. v9: "But the Lord God called out to Adam, "Where are you?" v10: He answered, `I heard you in the garden, and I was afraid, "Because I was naked; So I hid."v11: "And God said, "WHO "TOLD "YOU" that you were "NAKED? "Have you eaten from the tree, I "COMMANDED" you `NOT` to `EAT` FROM?"....`End Quote`....... "Adam and "Eve had taken a bite of the "Forbidden Fruit"..... "That "God `` "TOLD" HIM `` "NOT to "Partake of, "That was in the Garden,..."So, "Where Are You!.... "When God calls to you; "Are you Hiding, "Because" Of what someone told you.... ``"WHO "TOLD "YOU!!! "THAT YOU WERE "NAKED?!! "God knew the `Devil` had been talking to `Him`,... (just like he's talking to you in your `EAR`) don't let no one(`The Enemy`)tell you nothing about what you can't do, "Because, "God is now saying to you, "WHO TOLD YOU!!!... `You're not Qualified` "WHO "TOLD "YOU!!!, ``that you made too many mistakes`, "WHO "TOLD YOU!!! `That you will never be "SUCCESSFUL" `, "WHO "TOLD YOU!!!, `You came from the wrong family`,... "People have stopped chasing their "Dreams, and "Visions `` today, "Based upon what "SOMEONE ``"TOLD ``"THEM! "Now "God is asking "YOU!!!.... ("WHO "TOLD YOU), "That you couldn't be, "What you wanted to be, "WHO TOLD YOU!!! ..., "That you'll "NEVER" amount to nothing,

"WHO TOLD YOU!! "Just because you are not Born in "AMERICA" that your "DREAMS `.... `ARE!...`JUST!...`THAT!....dreams, "And you'll never have the chance to bring them to "Fruition, "To be able to have your "DREAMS" to "METAMORPHOSIS" itself into the wonderful creation that you saw in your "Mind,... "DREAMS" that one day you'll are able to help the people of America, or "The World Even, "WHO "TOLD "YOU!!! that you'll never be a "DOCTOR! a "LAWYER!... "WHO TOLD YOU" `Young MAN! `Young WOMAN! "Who is whispering in your `Ears, "Are you believing those "Negative "Voices, `That tell you to "STOP" your "DREAMING" and to stop having "VISIONS"... `Because, "It's never going to work,... "What `Voices` and `SPIRITS` "Are you listening to?.... "Is it telling you `That you can't get your "MASTER'S DEGREE"... "DON'T, allow the devil to continue to WHISPER in your EAR, "Telling you, "That you can't do This, or That,.... `OR` Completing your "EDUCATION"; WHO TOLD YOU!!! "That, `There "WILL" never be a "BLACK PRESIDENT"....`And, "WHO TOLD YOU" `That there will never be a "Woman" "VICE" "PRESIDENT"... "You have the "Ability to do "Anything that you want to do, `Once you tell your `MIND`, "YOU CAN DO".... ``Turn! The! Light! On!!! "The "Brain will feed off of Your "Positive Energy," `That you feed it`, "Whether it be `NEGATIVE! or "POSITIVE! ... "A lot of things that have happened in our lives, "That we've seen, "And "Heard ``... Things, `That would have us to be `FEARFUL` , `OF THE `FUTURE `, "The Expectations of "LIFE! ``Is going to be "SCARY!!! "Enough! "Especially from Hearing all the "NO's, and the `Let Downs`..."It'll start to work on your "WILLPOWER" after a while... "Witch you have to keep "STRONG": "Bad thoughts, "And thoughts of `Tiredness,. "Thoughts of, `You Just Can't Go On`... `Are the Wrong Voices to listen to, "Especially in the Morning's, "Because, "Mornings are the most important part of the day for you, "It's gonna `Direct` your `Day, `Depending` on how you start your `Day` of "THINKING"..... "I know a lot of people are going to say, "Why didn't it work for me? "Well, "It would have, "If I would have had someone there in the home when I was young, "To teach me to `Control` my `ANGER,... and `Controlling ` the way I "THINK" to `Control` My "EMOTIONS"...``To really break down how the devil is working against me, "Through my own "Head ``... "And that nothing, `Is, "Never what it Appears to be, "And to always keep my "FAITH STRONG"... `By Practicing the Principles of Faith,.... "Faith in the "Lord "Jesus "Christ, "Repentance, "Baptism," And receiving the gift of the Holy Ghost..... "When I was young, (Mr. Steve Harvey said it the best) I was doing a lot of, `What we call today "HOPING`... `Little did I know, "I was putting my "FAITH" to work, "At that time......"That's all what "HOPING" is.... "FAITH,"...."Look"....HOPING=FAITH .... "Every time you use the word "HOPE" you might as well say the word "FAITH" and use it as it reads, "FAITH"...( `So In your lifetime, `You might have said,...(STEVE HARVEY quotes) `Man I "HOPE" I get that "Job, "And you end up getting it, `end quote` ("Don't you understand that, "You've used the POWER of "FAITH!) "And didn't even know it"....That's the only way I can interpret these things to you my "Bredrin, "Now, "Thy `Eyes` are `Open, "To the Truth,"...."You see, "I didn't have a Father to tell me these things, "And break it down for me in Layman's terms, "That even a Dummy like me, "Can Understand"... " I lost out, "BUT," "I'm not saying it's too late, `I'm still in the game, "So `Son` Please learn from my `Mistakes`, "And from me, for "Not having the right "MINDSET" in my `YOUTH DAYS`, "That I have Now, "BECAUSE" if I did, "It would be "ON LIKE DONKEY KONG"... "But I'm on the right track "NOW".... "I'm just saying, "I would have had something to pass it to you Son, and Grandson,... "And, like I said it's not too late for "Me ``I'm not throwing in the towel yet"....And to whoever "Else, That "Can Relate," "And Learn"........"Now, "I've made my share of `Mistakes` in my lifetime, "But, "Mistakes are Not, "Mistakes" "When you have learned from them, "So I Encourage you to make Mistakes, `So that you can learn from them,... "The only way! "You knew, two plus two = four was to write down three, "And the

Teacher corrected you, "But".... "The Mistake, "Was, "Will Learned," So I'm not Actually hating on `Mistakes, "Because we need them, `In order to Learn`, `To Progress`, "To Go To The Next Level," "BUT, we don't want to continue to make the "SAME MISTAKE" `Because, then you become `Annoyed`, `And then your "Enthusiasm" for the "Truth" Starts to Decline`, And your not caring anymore about the situation at hand...." So, "Always start your day with positive thoughts, "like I will be "SUCCESSFUL," I will "ACCOMPLISH" all my "GOALS" "TODAY,"..... "But, "Those! "Wrong Voices," `That is talking to you...LIKE` ,"You need to `Chill` out Today..... "I am weak," "I am afraid," "Just "Negative "Thoughts, "After "Negative "Thoughts...." Put! "Positive! "Thoughts in your head, "When thoughts tell you, "You're just Average," "There's Nothing Special about you, "Get rid of that DEFEATED thought, "And think "POWER" Thoughts, "I am "FEARFULLY" and "WONDERFULLY" Made..."I AM A "MASTERPIECE," "I "Have "Royal Blood" Flowing! Through My "Veins"... "I am "CROWNED" with the "Favor of "God"...."So always Pray your Day Through, "By praying every Morning, "Asking "God to "ORDER" your "STEPS" to take "CONTROL" of your "DAY" So that Nothing happens by `Chance`... "So Pray, "To make your day `Prosperous`, "By feeding your `Mind` with POSITIVE Thoughts, "From the "BEGINNING" of your "DAY," `Like` taking the `Word,` "I CAN'T" out of your "VOCABULARY"....,"All that's doing is `DRAINING` you of your `STRENGTH` of `POSITIVITY`..."You're going to Discover, like I did, "You're going to need `Strength, "STRENGTH" you didn't know you Had, "You Needed "God's "Strength, and "Grace... It's going to help you to do what you didn't think you could do, "You need to "Power "Up, "Get your mind going in the right "Direction when you wake up, `By saying things like, "This is going to be a `Good Day`, "I can Handle "Anything that "Comes my Way Today, "I am Strong "I Am Confident," I have the Favor of "God, "And he "WILL" send "ANGELS" to watch over me..... "I'm Excited about my Future now, "At the start of the day, "You need to set your

Mind for Victory," Don't let just Any, `Thought` Play, "You have to think thoughts on "Success, "If you wake up, `And just think, "WHATEVER"....`Your mind will tell you, ``That you have too many problems`` "You're too tired,..."You'll never overcome these Obstacles` "Nothing good is going to happen today` "If you don't set the tone for the day!! "NEGATIVE" "THOUGHTS" will set in, "So before you check your phone, "Before you read your email, "Before you go to see what the weather is like, "You need to start thinking on "POSITIVITY" and "Power" thoughts of "Victory! "Thoughts of "ABUNDANCE!.... "Psalm 125 says; "God, will be good to those who are in `Tune` with him: "You say how can I be in tune with him, "By thinking "VICTORIOUSLY," overcoming the "BAD SITUATION," "If you go around thinking I'll never get well, "This Depression," "This Anxiety" "This Stress" is going to hinder me all of my life, "Unfortunately you're not in `Tune` with "God, "And you won't find "God" `Anywhere`, "As long as you continue to think NEGATIVE…,"You can only find God by thinking; "Victoriously, and "Faithfully, "IF you go around thinking I'll never Get `WELL` "This `Depression`, "This Addiction is going to stop me,... "Well then, "God" wouldn't be able to help you... "Because of your "Negative Thoughts".... "THE "GOD, that you "SERVE"… .,"Said"..."I AM".... "GOD"...."I AM, "ALL POWERFUL "..., "I SPOKE WORLD'S into "EXISTENCE".... "I FLUNG STAR'S! into SPACE,"God said, MY name is "I AM, "I AM "LIGHT, "I AM, "PROVISION, and "I AM "ABUNDANCE,... "You get `Favor` from "God" "You've got `Favor` for life, And "God's "Favor ain't "Fair..."It's just like you, and your "Son"... I'm pretty sure, `You would do anything for him, "And Sometimes, `You may even turn a blind `Eye` to some of his wrong doings, `That... You wouldn't do for others, "That's the type of Favor you need with"God ``… "The same Favor he had with "King "David... "But that's another book that I would like to talk about with you soon, "By the Grace of "GOD"......"GOD said in the Beginning, ``Let there be light, "And it came at a "Hundred and "Eighty "Six "Thousand "Miles "Per. "Sec. ("I RESEARCHED IT") When you think about that, ("ACTUALLY") it's really hard to even Conceive of, or "To even think about, "This is how "Powerful the "GOD" we serve is,...So, "Son, "Another thing I want to talk to you about, "Is writing your "VISIONS" "Down on a piece of paper, "And your "Expectations, and "Dreams, `A Checklist, "That you wish to "Fulfill in your "Lifetime, "It's very Important".... "And I just found out this just recently, "And it makes "Perfect Sense"......"This is Important, "One reason being, "If you read something every day, "You become "CONSCIOUS" of it, "And your SPIRIT will DESIRE to have it to "MANIFEST".... "Scriptures Say" In Habakkuk 2:2–3 says: To, "Write the Vision, "And make it plain upon tables, "That he may run, that readeth it. v3: For the Vision is yet for an appointed time, "But at the end it shall speak, "And not lie: "Though it tarry, Wait for it; "Because it will surely come, "It will not tarry. (that word tarry means even though it's taking a long time) wait for it... for surely, it will come at the appointed time; "GOD, "Don't say nothing, he don't make come true, Once "YOU" believe in your "Dreams and "Visions, "That you been Praying about... "Hey, It's already in route to you, "That Promotion you've been believing in, "You may not see any signs of it"YET, ``,"But what you can't see, "IS "GOD "Behind " Scenes! "He is moving the "WRONG PEOPLE" out of your way, "And the "RIGHT PEOPLE" in your way..."GOD'S, moving things in your "Favor"... ``Lining up the "Breaks you need, `Remember`,..."God didn't bring you this far to leave you, "And though you may have `Big`Challenges, "We Serve a "BIG "GOD,"..... "Dreams may look Impossible, "But GOD! "Can do the "IMPOSSIBLE," "Even though, "You have no Clue, "On what's going to happen to "US,"...`Or how it can happen for "US,"..."But in the blink of an eye, "Things can `Change` for you, "" If you use the Power of "POSITIVE THINKING," .."You're going to "Haft to love yourself, "Before any of the "Principles of Faith" `Can work for you! "I cannot express that "Enough! "Keeping GOD! "First in your life.... "I know you can't make it to Church every Sunday... "But..... "You Can"... "Because `Church` is "ANYWHERE" and "EVERYWHERE" you feel `YOU ` need" to talk to "GOD" …"Basically what I'm saying is to, "Be a Godly Man, and "PRAY, "PRAY," PRAY,…"No matter where you are, "Pray your Day Through," "Always ask "God to "ORDER your "STEPS for Today, "So then, "You'll know, "That nothing by `Chance`, "Is just going to Occur today… "And all the good things that happen today, "Was Ordered by God"… "And" Yes," Even the `Bad.` "That's why I do not believe in good luck, or bad luck, "Because, "If your praying and believing in, "GOD `` to "Direct your "Path, "So whatever happens to you throughout that day, "Is Ordered by "GOD ``…. "So what does good luck, or bad luck has to do with it, "And always speak goodness on yourself, "There is "POWER" in the tongue! "So don't curse yourself, "What I mean by that is," Never say I am Broke! "You say, I'm in between blessings, don't claim that curse of `BROKENNESS` on yourself, "And right now I'm talking to everyone out there, "MEN and WOMEN" "God's very reason for waking you up EVERYDAY, Is because GOD ain't finished with you yet, "Or you wouldn't wake up, "Because, "HE still has something for you to do,.." But you have to start living your life in "EXPECTATION!!! you have to start "EXPECTING!!! great things to happen for you, "IN order for it to "HAPPEN, "IT is the law of "Attraction"… `It is real what the `WORD` says, "About a Man: It says; "A Man is, As he "THINKETH" ``"If you live your life in "EXPECTATIONS"….. "Expecting good Things to happen to you, Well, "Rest Assured, "AND" BELIEVE that good things ARE going to happen, "Because, you "WILL" them to. "Now on the other hand" `If you live your life in "DESPAIR", and thinking NEGATIVE, "Nothing good is going to happen ……. "And Women," "IF YOU SAY", "That all Men are Dogs ``,"You're Going To Meet Every Last One Of Them, "Because that's the way you're thinking, "AND IF YOU SAY, "I'll never be Rich!… "Chances are, "YOU WANT" "But the moment you Change the Frequency in your head, "And the way you think, "Different things start to come back to you, "And you start to remember things, "But you gotta be careful in how you say things out aloud, "Because, `The evil one is listening also, To everything you say, "And he will make bad things manifest! "I always tell "Myself Aloud" that, "Goodness and "Mercy shall follow me "All" the days of my life!! "As the Psalmist says in Psalms…." I know that you're working for someone SON, "And I know you got a lot of ideas for yourself, "Big Ideas" `So, "Opening up your "IMAGINATION";…. "And explore "New Content, "And "New `Ideas` on `Business `Adventures`, "Because," You don't want to work for someone all your life, "That's why I said earlier, "It's good to have Friends, "THAT also have "BIG IMAGINATIONS" "DREAMS"and "VISIONS" because it'll rubs off on you, "GOD" talks to us through your `IMAGINATION` and he shows you things, "New Inventions" "New Ideas" on the `Future`…. "But you gotta be very careful on sharing your "IMAGINATION"…. "BECAUSE"….. "GOD" didn't show it to Nobody but "You! "So how could they Understand what "You See" inside of "YOUR IMAGINATION"…… "So halftime when you share with them, What you might have `IMAGINED` they think you going crazy, `The problem with Sharing your `IMAGINATIONS` with others is,….. `We share it to the wrong people, "People, that are blind to your "IMAGINATION" your `DREAMS and VISIONS`…." IF, "Mr. MARTIN COOPER, would listen to anybody other than his `OWN MIND`, We would never have a "CELL PHONE" today, "He is the INVENTOR of the cell phone, "But God gave him a "Vision a "Dream….. "And look, "Today we are walking around with his "IMAGINATION"…. "Do you know who "VINTON CERF" and "BOB KAHN" is…. "We'll, "These are the Gentleman that are Credited for "INVENTING" the "INTERNET" they are the brains behind the information superhighway, is an intricate set of protocols and rules that someone had to develop before we can get the World Wide Web. "Before the current Iteration of the Internet, "long-distance Networking between Computers was first Accomplished in a 1969 Experiment by two Research teams at `UCLA` and `STANFORD UNIVERSITY`… "And let's not forget "JEFF BEZOS ``of "Amazon `` Is an American entrepreneur, "Who played a key role in the growth of e-commerce as the "Founder" and "Chief "Executive Officer of Amazon, Worth over $180 Billion Dollars today…. "What if these "MEN," `Would have listened to "Anything or "Anybody else `` Other than their own "IMAGINATIONS" and their own "DREAMS"…. `Would we have the Technology, "And the things that we're using today from some of these Great Men, "I Don't think so…."IF you want to kill a Big Dream, "Tell it to a small Minded Person, "Do you know how many times God has shown you something, "In your "IMAGINATION" that was just for you to see, `at "THIS" time`, `It was just for you,…"You were so "Excited" when it came to "YOU!… "And when you shared it with your "Family! and "Friends!… "What they do, "They shot it down, "Why did they shoot it down though! "Because They Couldn't See It, or Understand it "And you know why they couldn't see it!! "Because, "God Didn't Show It To Them, "He showed it to You" "He showed you the Evidence, of Things Not Seen;…. "Your "Family and "Friend's may love you," But they don't know what GOD has in store for you…" What I'm trying to say is, "You have to be careful, "When you share your "IMAGINATION" with `SMALL-MINDED` People," Nobody else can see your IMAGINATION but "YOU"… "It ain't just you `IMAGINING` stuff, "It's GOD showing you a free upcoming attraction of things to come,…."That he has for you," And possibly the "World; "Though you…. "God has you right where he wants you,… "You're in the `PROCESS` right now of Becoming what GOD wants you to be, "He's the reason we wake up everyday, "Because God ain't through with us yet, "That should be pretty clear, "Because He still has something for us, "That we've yet to receive, "But you have to start living your life with "Expectation! "You have to start Expecting!!"`GREAT" things to happen to you, in order for `Great` things to happen for you, "You ain't got to be, "GREAT" to get started, "But you got to get started to be "GREAT `` "Those words from the great "Les Brown"… Now, To all you young people out there in the world, ` With All of the "Extraordinary Capabilities," You have to decide if you are willing to do the things that it takes, "To put you in that category, "People listen up`` "This is just a `Suggestion` "To the youth in this world today, "DON'T do what I did, "And most people I know, "Mess up life, In all of their "Twenties," `And "From the age of `twenty, "To the age of `twenty-nine, "We just missed those years right up! lol, Because `twenty is that age where you are; "Just trying to have "FUN ``... `You're free` and maybe just out of "High School," "And you don't live at your `Mama's house `Anymore ``You're out on my own, `And what do we do…. "Statistics says that 98 percent of us in our `Twenties,` Are trying to exert ourselves` In the `FUN` Category……"We got to get off work, "So we can go ge "HIGH ``….. "You got to get off work, "So we can go and have A "DRINK"… "A COLD ONE!… "You Hurry to get off work, `To make it to "Happy Hour ``"You got to hang out with the `Fellas, "You gotta go play `Video Games`…."The average person blows all of their `twenty years, "And then you start to notice, "Time ain't waiting for you, "It's too late,…. "NOW you're in your thirties…. "And now guess what happens to you, "Including MySelf, "I spend all of my thirties, "Trying to do the things, "That I should have been doing in my `twenties, "So now my life is "Behind" TIME"… "Now and we're in your forties`` "And you're still trying to do the "Things," And have the "Things, `That you could have had in your thirties,… "Had I just done the things, `That I was Supposed to do in my thirties, and then the Tragedy sets in, "You look up, "And you're fifty, "Now that doesn't mean that is too late` "Because, "Surely it's not too late for me, ("I'M NO FOOL "NO SIREE, "I'M GOING TO LIVE TO BE, "A HUNDRED AND THREE!!!) A lot of you guys are too young to know where that slogan came from, (Hmmmm)… "And now all of a sudden, "You're are trying to create a life for yourself, that you could have created, "When you was in your thirties`` `My suggestion to all young people, "Don't Do What I Did" `And mess up your "Twenties"; "Those ARE SOME VERY IMPORTANT DAYS OF YOUR LIFE," "IS YOUR TWENTIES," IF I had a Chance to do it all over again, "I would BUCKLE down in my "TWENTIES," while you're YOUNG and ENERGETIC …"Because, "I feel that it is the part of your life that you need to be in "FULL BEAST MODE" in creating a life that you `Desire`… "And making a Situations for yourself; "And fine tuning your road to `SUCCESS`…. "Because,`Your twenties are your `DEDICATION` Years, A time in your life that Whatever you Believe In, "You'll be "DEDICATED" to it, "You'll give "COMMITMENT`,…. "COMMITTING yourself to whatever causes you believe in, "It's about being `DEDICATED` to the 'Right Things' though, "So don't do like I did"…. I was `DEDICATED` to the "Wrong Things, "like the Girls, "Going out with my Boys, "The Video Games, "The Clubs," Happy Hour, "The Smoke, "The Drinks, "The "TEMPTATIONS" of our `Desires`……."But being `Dedicated` to our `Desires, "Locks us out of our very Purpose in Life, "So the twenties are a very important time, "In a Man's life, "But you see that's how the "Devil" WORK`……."He also knows a Man's "Highest Potential" of his "MEMORIZATION" and "COMMITMENT" is at "Hand," "That's when he can do the most `DAMAGE` during the age of his twenties to thirties …. "So, "You should be in full "BEAST MODE" to "SUCCESS" in your twenty years of age, "By the time you're thirty, "You should finish with Drinking and the Partying, "And Smoking, "And more than one `Relationship` at the same time, "We have to Alleviate some of the `Stuff` that we showed `DEDICATION` to in our Twenties, 'You don't want lock yourself out of the "AMERICAN DREAM"…… "That's why the devil is after our ``Young People``… "Haven't you "Noticed" that their either "Locked Up," Homeless, or Alcoholic, or Drug Deals, Addict, "The devil knows how to take our young people away from us" And he knows how to "RUIN CAREERS" `If he can get you `Early in your `Life, "He will Ruin every Chance you have of "SUCCESS"…… "Look, "I ain't Nobody, "I'm just trying to share some `Valuable `Information, "Because, "I've been "THERE and "DID "THAT, "And lived the messed up side of life, "It was a struggle, `With only a twelfth-grade `Education` out of school, 'Married' and "Divorced," "Losing everything I ever had, "Going to "Prison"…….. "I did so many `Things `Wrong, `And made so many `Mistakes... "BUT" "God" has blessed me to `Bounce `Back,..... "And you can bounce back, "But you gotta want to bounce back, "Because the devil is going to continue ride your back, "And throw "OBSTACLES" in your way,.... "You now what they say; "If it ain't one thing" "It's another"..... Whatever you're doing right now to SUCCEED in LIFE , "You got to Quadruple it, "And; `When you "THINK! `You've done all you can, "And you can't do no more... "THEN" GET BUSY".... "You know, "I kind of see `Life` now, "Like a `Movie`, "with every position on the set, played by (me)or, you, ("well in that case you") "You're the "Director," You're the Writer, "The Actor," The Producer,.... "What I'm trying to say is, "If there's something going on in your life, "That you don't like.... "WELL THEN! "Erase the movie!" "And CHANGE "IT! "You have the "Ability" to CHANGE"YOUR" life,..."To CHANGE who "YOU are, "REWRITE IT!... Rewrite your "LIFE," Change the SCRIPT!..."CHANGE the ACTORS if you have to, "And! "What I mean by that is, "The People in your Life, "That are "Weighing you down, " Get rid of them, "Because you don't want "Anything, ``or "No one! "Slowing you down from your "Next Endeavors" ... "Who you align yourself up with, "Is going to Determine your Future, "So `Walk` with the "WISE! "And Become "Wise!..."Because if you don't, `You'll Surely Sinks to the Bottom. "Just like Everybody else has, "Who Didn't "CHANGE" their life Around; "Re-write your `Story` of Life, "If it's not going well for you "Now!.... "Hire "New Actors, `If the ones that you have, "Are not "Sufficient!,..... "Find New Ones," "Because, "You can't be walking around with a group of Friends that always comes to you with their problems, "There's no room for You to `Grow`, "And if they "ARE doing it, "That's Because they see something in "YOU, "They can see that you're more `Balance` and `Stable`.... "But you have to remember this," There is an old saying, "If you're the smartest person in your group"... "You need a new group! "You cannot be the `GO` to person in the group; "YOU CAN'T; "And `Expect to `SUCCEED; at the same... "But don't worry about it, "Because that means that you have a "GIFT" In `Solving Problems`… "You can earn a lot of Money Solving People's Problems, "You know people pay for this in other Countries,…." And in this Country as well"…… "They pay for `Expert `Advice, "The Moment you become a "Expert in something in "AMERICA," `You can make a "Million Dollars "EASILY, "All you gotta to do is become an "EXPERT," "At `ONE` thing in life," And you got it made in the `shade` "But like I was saying earlier, "Pay Close "Attention to the "Ones that are in "Your "Circle, "You haft to have yourself, A `Special` group of `Friends, "That'll be down for You, "When you need them, "And You for `Them, "When they Need You … "So, "Choose wisely" "Because I can promise you, "That you'll have some that will turn on you, "It's going to be so many people in this world, `That's not going to `Believe in you, "But while you're sitting around worrying about people liking "US"…. "Why don't you "Focus on Believing in "OURSELVES! "And our "GOALS"…. "And `live life"…. "That's what it's about, "YOU"….. "Why do we run? "Are we "RUNNING for a `Reason`, "Do you even understand the "Purpose `behind your "RUN" …. "And `Why` are you running, "Do you have "Enough` "Faith, in "WHY" you're "RUNNING!," Are you afraid you're going to "FAIL" at Something! "Do you have `Enough "Faith to "RUN" FASTER, "Are you Prepared to test your "Faith, "let me ask you something, "How "Fast can you "Run! "Maybe we have to slow down sometime, "Because when you cut some corners," You got to `Understand, "There are some `Unique` `Obstacles` that `Awaits you, "Are you `Prepared to "RUN through `THEM! "Are you `Prepared to "RUN `Faster! "Are you `Prepared to "RUN `Stronger! "Do you Understand what it means to "RUN" towards your "GOALS, "Many people started "RUNNING" towards something, "And don't have the "TENACITY to even `Finish, "You may have to take your time a little bit, `When you First get `Started, "But, "Sooner or later, "You got the pick up the pace, "You got to "START! "Moving` A little bit "FASTER, "And you got to have a "Desire for "Something that'll "Make you "RUN Faster!, `But "UNDERSTAND! that it's gonna "Requires

"CARRIAGE" as you "Start to "RUN" FASTER, "And when you feel Yourself Start to get a Little "Tired`, "And when you Start feel that you "DON'T have "ENOUGH left! "Here's a CLASSIC! "SUGGESTION".....";DIG DEEPER! "And" RUN! FASTER! "You've got to be the ONE to make it to the "FINISH LINE! "And even when you cross the FINISH LINE, "PREPARE `Yourself for the "Next "Race of your "LIFE!! "Have you got a "PLAN" ..."Where are you," RUNNING? `Are you "RUNNING for a `Reason`, "Do you know the purpose behind your "Run! "Do you have `Enough "FAITH in your "RUNNING!,"Are you afraid of what you may Encounter, "Do you have "Enough "TALENT, "Are you prepared to test your "TALENTS...... "Can you "RUN `` .... "Now, "You got to slow down sometimes `Thou`," So that you can turn the corner of "SUCCESSFULNESS" ,"Many people "Runaway"...,"Instead of `Facing! their "Fears and "Endeavors..... "So don't `Run for Nothing, "Don't `Run for `Stats `,"BUT "RUN "Because you know it's "Necessary "BUT "Understanding, "ENDURANCE is "Required," "So don't let "Dead weight slow you down, "Because, `Dead Weight`, `Is just that! "DEAD" it has no life, "But YOU have "LIFE! "So you must continue your "PLIGHT" and your ENDEAVORS to "SUCCESS, "And if you feel you're getting a little "Tired, "I "Suggest you go into the "Next Gear!, "I suggest you go into "Second and "Third Gear," Push it into "Overdrive "Push it into "G. "Forces, "But Running towards a "VICTORY, "Towards the "OPPORTUNITIES" "Toward your "VISIONS" and "GOALS" "And always be a "FINISHER" of Whatever you "Started`,..."You take "QUITTIN" Out! your "Vocabulary, "It is "NOT" an "OPTION" nor a "SELECTION,""But" RUN!!! With a "Full "HEART!! "Run!! with everything you have in your "Heart and "Soul, "Now I know some days are going to be slow, "But you gotta tell yourself to pick up the pace a little bit "But we have to make sure we're "Running with the "Right "Mind "Set, "RUNNING! Towards our "Goals....." I've heard someone say, "That is okay for your `Pockets` to be "Broke! "As long as your "MIND" makes "SENSE!...... "I can kind of see that` Because, if your Mind makes "Sense, "And you know! "It makes "Sense, "That means you know the "VALUE" of your "WORTH ` "And "That's "the main" GOLD .... "LEARNING" "And knowing you're `Worth, "And what you're capable of,"But you gotta use a little "HOPE! and some "FAITH! "Oh Yeah! "It's going to take some effort on your part as well, "A little bit of work! "Anything that's worth having,"Is worth putting your time into, "You Feel Me" "And, A lot of times,"We have to rationalize, "And talk to ourselves," Don't worry," Nobody will hear you,..."But it is good to give yourself a Analyzation every now and then, "To keep yourself up to Par" "And" HONEST ``... "Because good things are "SUPPOSED" to happen to you;?"The Word of GOD say... .. "Goodness and Mercy shall follow me all the days of my life: "So you can't be Drifting off," And start to thinking that, "Bad things are supposed to happen to you, "Every Morning," "You should start your "Day Off" every day" By "Saying: "GOOD THINGS ARE SUPPOSED TO HAPPEN TO ME TODAY" Because God also said in "JOB 22:28" "Thou shall also "Decree a "Thing, "And it shall be "ESTABLISHED" unto thee; "And a light shall shine on your way:... "So that "Means, "To Speak the Words into "EXISTENCE" until they "MANIFEST"..... "You need to "WATCH `` your"WORDS ``.... "And what you say about yourself, Because words have "POWER `` and"MEANING `` in them, "So don't "CURS yourself, By saying I'm `Broke`... "Say, I'm between "Bank "Transactions, "Anything but I'm "Broke, "Because you'll be just that.... "BROKE"..... "If you keep saying it, "like I said early in this book, "The" Egyptians, or "DOCUMENTED," `TO be the Smartest Generation known to `MAN yet,(Hmmmmm) "And they were doing "Fantastic" things with the "MIND" that most of us are unable to Duplicate today, "But "God" said, "IN His Word" That he made "Every "Man "Equal: "So that means that there's "NO "Differences "BETWEEN" "THEM" and "US" we are just not Digging Deep Enough, `To get in touch with our Souls and Minds, `As they did,.... "To bring out the POWER of "GOD" that's within us, "listen we have more" POWER" in our baby "FINGER" then you will ever "Realize, "it's like this! "God said: In his word "That he made "MAN IN HIS OWN IMAGE: "So that means!, "We are Baby gods;" But we're, just not able to tap into the "Power as we "Pleased, "I'm sure you read about people bumping their heads," And all of the sudden," They can see into the future, or "A person bursting, "A pair of handcuffs, "Did you know it takes 500 pounds of pressure to snap a pair of handcuffs, "And it's recorded that `MAN` has done this, "So why is any other man, "Any different, "From the other, "God said I made all "MAN" "EQUAL" If one can see into the `Future, "Then other man can see into the "Future, "And `Bust a pair of handcuffs, "You see there's different Levels of "CONSCIOUSNESS, `In our BRAIN that, Allows us to do certain things, at certain "TIMES…, "Like a bad accident may have happened in someone's life, "Like bumping their head, "And going into a Coma, "And coming out of it with "Strange Abilities," "That you didn't have before the Coma, "But my thing is this, "God said that he made "MAN" in his own "IMAGE"…… "So that means we have certain "POWERS "ALSO, "But the only "Difference is, "The `CONDITIONING` of the `MIND: `When you are "BORN`," You are taught that; "You as a "Human Being" "CANNOT" "FLY `` … (OOPS there's that "WORD" again ("CAN'T") "So…"You will "NEVER" "FLY" "Because your `MIND` is not `Condition to "FLY"……."BUT!!!! I BEG THE DIFFER `` the" MONKS ``"are" FLYING!!!…. "They may Not be Flying, or Soaring through the Air, "But they are "Floating "Off the "Ground, "And "THAT'S, A "FORM of "FLYING," They're just not soaring through the sky, "But they're "Floating; "So they're `Flying `Basically, "So if the monks are doing it, "Why can't you or me do it, "Because, It's called "CONDITIONING" of the "MIND"………."You are working with an "UNCONDITIONED," and "UNTRAINED" `MIND`, "So you will "NEVER FLY," "But my thing is this, "God said, "That HE made every Man `EQUAL`;.."There is nothing `HE or `SHE can do, "That "I" CAN'T do, "You just have to "RECONDITION" your "MIND" stop limiting yourself, "By saying "I "CAN'T"....."BECAUSE, after that, "You basically have killed the Motivation for anything to Manifest; "Preventing the Chance, "Of you "SUCCEEDING" in your "ENDEAVORS" that You were trying to Succeed in; `You've killed it, `You "HAVE" to take "CAN'T" out of your "VOCABULARY" AND put words like "I CAN"... "I WILL" ... "We have to start "IMPEDING" on a "Higher sense of "OURSELVES".... ``Going to "New ``Levels `` "But we have to ``Understand that, "New "Levels, "Brings New devil's..... "But the time is "Right, "The stage is "Set...... "You're a MIRACLE looking for a `Place to "HAPPEN," "Don't let anybody tell you you're too `Young`, "Don't let anybody tell you you're too `Old`, "When you wake up in the "Mornings, "You tell yourself, "That the Best Is Yet To "Come,"...... "Tell Yourself," "THIS IS MY MOMENT" and I'm "DETERMINE to "Live it,..... "The Mind Is The "Battleground"..... "The fight is in your Mind, "Are you ready for the `Next Level`,....."What are `YOU` going to do with the `Time` you have `Left`, "You now when I was a teenager, I thought I knew it `ALL`, "But when I got a Chance to put it all into "ACTION," "To put it in "PERSPECTIVE," I suddenly found out, "That it wasn't going to be easy as I thought it would be, `And if you live long `Enough, "You will find out, "That life has a way of "SHUTTING" you "DOWN,".... "IT'LL!! Make "You......" Close...... "Your..... "MOUTH," "It will find a way to "MUTE" YOU," "That's why `Sometimes`, "I even question the "Technology," I really don't Need Another way for Anyone to Access Me, "All of the "Calls, "All of the text messages, "All the `Emails`, "Because sometimes we just get "OVERWHELMED".... "OVERWHELMED" by life "ITSELF," "All of the "STRUGGLES," "THE DEMANDS, "AND yes the "TEMPTATIONS," "It won't be long before "YOU" start to feel OVERWHELMED by life,.... "KNOW WHO YOU ARE," "So no one can "TRICK" you into being `SOMEONE` your not, "Because, If you "Know WHO YOU ARE," "THEN YOU KNOW WHO YOU'RE "NOT"!,.... "You can `Decide` that you're going to stand up to life, "And use your "Pain to "Push you to "Greatness, "And if you Fail," "Try "Again! and "Again! and "AGAIN!! "Because, "This is "Not the End you "Yet!, "And if you Fall Down, "Try to land on your back, "Because, "If you can look Up," "You can get Up," "And "Remember this, "If you're going through the "Hard "Times," Remember this,.... "IT DID NOT COME TO STAY," "IT CAME TO PASS," `Now the Enemy is going to through everything he has at you, `In your path, "Trying to trip you up, "You see his `Objective is to get you to stop `Whatever YOU'RE trying to do, "Or put together, "Just Remember This"..... "Nobody can Stop You," "But You"...... "YOU! have to be The "ONE" to say I "Give Up"...., That you're Turning Out the "Light Switch," "No one can Turn it Off, "But You," "Don't allow it to happen, "God said he would "Never "Leave "You, "Nor "Forsake "You," "Don't let the world "CONVINCE" you that you're `A `NOBODY, `"Because you are "SOMEBODY"...."You just don't know it yet, "I'm speaking to the Champion in you, "Get back up, "Don't let life defeat you, "You're `STRONGER` than that, "Your made in GOD'S image, "Know what that "Means!, "You need to Understand the Power that you Possess, "Because, "If you don't understand it, "It won't work for you, "You're a "WINNER,"" A "WARRIOR," "You were "Designed" for the "STRUGGLE," "So when you "FALL," And believe me, "You will "FALL," NO one can do it on their first try, "But you need to get back up, "And Continue to "STRUGGLE," Have a Deep Desire to "WIN," "And to "CLIMB," "You can tell when someone's ready to go to the "Next Level," "Because, "You see it in their "EYES," "You need to "CLIMB" when the whole world Calls you CRAZY, "You need to start "CLIMBING" when your `Friends and `Family say you'll never make it, "You see "WARRIORS" are "OVERCOMER" they know how to "CLIMB".... "Are you a "WARRIOR" can you "OVERCOME" the the "ATROCITIES" and the problems, "That life is going to throw at you, "You're gonna have to put your foot down, "And say nothing is going to stop me from being the `Man that "GOD wants me to be, "As an `AIR` to the "PROMISES" of "GOD,".... "We were given an "INHERITANCES," "Beyond our Capability to get on our own, "In order to received "INHERITANCES," "IT'S going to require "FAITH" , "And I mean some "STRONG FAITH,"..... GOD is not a "LIAR," "His word will not come back `VOID`..... BELIEVE and you will "RECEIVE," "Ask and it shall be "Given to "You, "Knock" And the "Door," shall "OPEN," it's just that easy, "You have to Believe though, "That He will can make it "Happen," "I believe there's three type of people in this world, "Those in the "Game`, "And those on the "Sideline," "And those in the stand "Watching," "You have to decide, "Which one of those "Three" You want to be, "You need to "CLIMB,"..... "CLIMB" "When the whole world tells you that your dream is too "Big,...."CLIMB," "When they turn their backs on you, "CLIMB," "When they tell you,"That you're "UNQUALIFIED" "CLIMB," "When your "Family doesn't believe in you, "CLIMB," "When "TEMPTATION" is knocking at your `Door`... "You need to "CLIMB," "When you start getting tired, "That's! when you really start to "CLIMB" even "HARDER!, "CLIMB," for every "NO" that `Someone` has told you, "CLIMB," "When your "Peers and "Teachers, Say, "I don't think he's going to make it, "CLIMB," "TO, go to the "NEXT LEVEL" "CLIMB" through "ADVERSITIES" "CLIMB" through your "ATROCITIES" "CLIMB" when everything around you seems to be "COMING" down, "DAY after "DAY..... "CLIMB" "When! you start to think that `IT'S` your "Last "Breath, "CLIMB,"......."You can always tell when someone's ready to go to the "Next Level," "Because, "You can see "IT "IN "THEIR "EYES,......"Tell yourself that you're "BLESSED" and "UNSTOPPABLE" in your "CLIMB," "And no one's going to stop "ME" but "ME".... "I am BLESSED and "HIGHLY" "FAVORED".... "I am a "KING" and will be treated and "RESPECTED" as "ONE," ....."That's the way you have to start thinking,.... "LIKE" A "WINNER,"... "We've got to Change your Mindset, "You have to start Thinking "BIG," to be "BIG" in STATUE,... Even the `WORD` says, "You are as you "Thinketh, "So if you start `Acting like a "KING" and "Respecting "Yourself as a "King" everybody else will, "Because, "If you

"Can't" see it, "How do you "EXPECT" the people to see it, "You have to "Believe in "Yourself in order for `Someone `Else to `Believe in `You, "And it's the same with "RESPECT" if you don't "RESPECT" yourself, "How can anybody else "RESPECT" you, "Even if they say "BAD things about you BEHIND your BACK, "BUT" in (YOUR)"PRESENCE" give you "BIG" "RESPECT" because they know that's how you "CARRY" "YOURSELF".... "DAMN" What they SAY `behind` your "BACK" but when there before you, "IT'S ALL"RESPECT ``...... "They only can `SEE` `YOU`, "The way you `SEE` "YOURSELF,"(HMMMMM). "You gotta ask yourself, "What do I want out of "Life," "What do you want out of a "Job," "What do you want out of a "CAREER," "What do you want out of a "RELATIONSHIP," "What gives you your "LIFE," "How will you know when you "GOT IT," "What will make you "HAPPY," "You need to "KNOW," "You need to start asking yourself some "Questions, "What do I really "WANT," "You need to be "Exact about what you "Need out of "LIFE,"...... "Don't just say I want to be "COMFORTABLE" ,"You're not being clear to "Yourself," "What will make you "HAPPY," "How `WILL you know when you "Got "It,...."You need "EXPECTED" certain things to happen in your life, "And as you do that, "It will "Stimulate the "SUBCONSCIOUS" Mind, "Then you'll begin to find those things to identify with, "And once you begin to `Determine what you "Want," "Take the time to "Write It "Down, "Don't just think about it, "Write it "Down, "That's a "Subjective process that "Engages, your "SUBCONSCIOUS" "MIND"..... "Write it "Down, "Once you "Write it "Down, "Read it "EVERYDAY," "THREE" times a day, "Morning, "Noon and "Night, "That's important because, "What it will do, "It will "Cause you to "Focus, "It will "Cause you to "CONCENTRATE"...... "When that "Other! "CONVERSATION" is going on "IN YOUR HEAD" telling you what you cannot do it, "Telling you to "STOP," "What you're Doing! "IT WON'T WORK"... "But you have to make that "Conscious "Decision, `That you're going to go, `All Out`, "Full"

"Force," "And tell yourself that nothing can stop me, "Nothing but `Me`, "And as long as I keep my "Faith, `And Endure to the `End, "It would see me through, "FAITH," "What's walking by `sight, `If I can "SEE" it, "I can do it, "NO "NO "NO lot of people say, "If I can see, "I'll believe it, "No, "IF YOU BELIEVE IT," "Well then, "YOU CAN SEE IT, "And don't be `Disturbed, "Because no one else can see it, "That's not "UNUSUAL, "That is "ORDINARY, "But, "Because, "You want a `Different` kind of "Results in your life, "You've got to be willing to be "UNREASONABLE"...... "And If you want "UNREASONABLE" results," You must be willing to do the `Things` today `OTHERS "Won't do, "In order to have a "Things "TOMORROW," "That "OTHERS" Won't have, "We complain about so many things in life, "But we do so little about it,"Or" to change the situation, "If you believe there's something still in you to do, "Well put your foot down, "And do it, "Just like "NIKE" says, just do it, "Build a strong character of yourself, "And know your "Value" and "Worth," "And stay in the "Fight, "Because, `You're are a Prisoner of `FAITH`, "You have to be more "DETERMINED" then "What's trying to "STOP" you,..... "YOU" are your number "ONE SPONSOR," "You have to take care of yourself, "Especially if you believe there's something left in you to do. "You have to "STOP" listening to the inner voice, "Telling you to stop what you doing, "It's NO use, "It WON'T work, "As you do that, "That will Stimulate your Superconscious Mind,.... "Then you'll begin to find those things that you'll want out of life, "And once you begin to `Determine what you want to do in life, "Take the time to "WRITE IT DOWN," "Don't just think about it, "You need to "WRITE IT DOWN," "That is a "Subjective "Process that `Engages the `Subconscious `Mind, "WRITE IT DOWN," `Once you Write It it Down read it "THREE" times a "DAY," "Morning, "Noon, and "Night, "Why is that important, "Because, `What it will do, `It will cause you to focus and will keep you accountable on what you have going on, `It would cause you to "Concentrate" "WHEN THAT OTHER CONVERSATION" is going on in your "HEAD," "Telling you what you "CANNOT DO," Telling you all of the "IMPOSSIBILITIES" and all of the "ATROCITIES," and "SETBACKS" that you're going to endure, "Scaring you away from any Adventure that you had in your mind, "Sometimes you have to turn that enter you off, "And tell yourself you have a made up mind, I'm going to "DO THIS NO MATTER WHAT IT TAKES," "NO matter how many times I FELL, "I will keep "GOING" and "GOING"... `You might as well call me the Energizer Bunny, "He just keeps "GOING and "GOING and "GOING and "GOING, "I have to keep telling myself "THAT"........, `Tell yourself, "No matter where I am today, "It's NOT where I'm going to "STAY"....... "You have to be more "DETERMINED" than what's trying to stop you, "And believe me, `There's going to be a lot of `Obstacles thrown in your way, "That's why "Paul said in the `Bible`, "That you must have "FAITH" to call "FORWARD" those things that are "NOT" as though they "WERE,".... "He's telling you to believe in what you're doing, "Believe, "That this thing can happen for you, "BELIEVE" that "GOD" is working on your side, "BELIEVE" that you can do all things, "Through Christ Jesus who strengthens me, "And we have to learn to "DISCIPLINE" ourselves, "SOCRATES" `Says, "A "UNDISCIPLINED" life, "IS an "INSANE" life, "You have to `Resell "Yourself, "To "Yourself "EVERYDAY," Luke 12:34; `Says, "Where your Treasures is,"There will your "HEART" be also, "You got to have the "Faith, "To go AFTER what you "BELIEVE IN," "So that means you got to "BELIEVE" in yourself, "COMMIT" yourSELF to something, "A "UNCOMMITTED" life has no Direction," You have to make a "Important" "Decision" in your life, "You gotta "DECIDE, "I'M ... GOING ... TO ... DO ...THIS .... NO .... MATTER ... WHAT!... "That's why I say, `You gotta "COMMIT" yourself to something, "Most people don't keep their "COMMITMENTS" to their "COMMITMENTS," that's why we leave our "LIVES in `Poverty, "LIVES" of `Misery, "LIVES" of `UNHAPPINESS`, "SOCRATES" also said, `That a "UNCOMMITTED" life "ISN'T" worth living," You got to be "COMMITTED" through the "STORM," "And the "Rain, "The heartache and the "PAIN" and the "DISAPPOINTMENTS," "EVERYBODY" can `Dream It,.... "But it `Won't `Happen, "UNLESS, `You're "COMMITTED" to it,.... "You "CAN'T" get "People to "Believe in your "Dreams, "IF `You Don't "BELIEVE` "IT! "Yourself!... "If you "DON'T see it, "They're "NOT" Going to `See` it, "You got to put `TIME` in what you "BELIEVE" `In, "You have to be able to "Build" up your "DREAMS" and "VISIONS," "And just because you're in a bind right now, "Doesn't" mean it's "OVER," "Spread your wings, "And "FLY".... "Because!, "If there's a "WILL" there's a "Way,... "How great is your "WILL," "Are you trying to "Bounce "Back from "Something, "Well" "Get" "Going! "Those "DREAMS" and "VISIONS" aren't going to Manifest themselves, `So ,"When you feel like giving up, "Tell yourself, "I "Won't "Give "Up... "That I've came too "Far to "QUIT" "Now!,"And I can do more than I "THINK" I "Can!, "I can go "FURTHER" than I "THINK," I can have "MORE" than I "THINK" I "Can!, "We have to stop ``Blaming ``Somebody`` ``Else``, `Over, "WHAT" we don't have, "And go out there and get "SOME" "Ourselves!, "You'll "APPRECIATE" it "MORE!, "You'll take care of it better, "Because, "YOU'VE" "EARNED" it, "I CAN DO ALL THINGS THROUGH JESUS CHRIST WHO STRENGTHENS ME, "He's taught me, "If I Start "SOMETHING," "I Need To Finish It," ("AND "THAT'S "FACTS") "I've have to say "YES,"... "YES to my "DREAMS," "YES to "ME,... "YES I "CAN,"... "Doesn't matter how many `Failures` I've made in life, "Doesn't matter what I've "DONE" in life, I can make it "HAPPEN,"... "There's going to be some "CHALLENGES," "And there's going to be some "TESTS," "BUT I've "Got to "Get "UP! "AND" "When it comes a "Time, "When I Want to "Stop! "And Give Up! "And believe me, "You will have those "Times, "And those "MOMENTS," "But that's "MY"FUEL "MY "GAS"! "MY "OCTANE" ``That I will turn it into my WHY'S...."My "WHY'S are gonna give me that edge that I need, "MY" "WHY'S" are going to give me the "ADVANTAGE" I need, "My "WHY'S,"...., "AS

I talked about earlier in the "BOOK,.... "WHY," my "CURIOSITY" always get the better of me, "I need to know "WHY,"... "Every time I run up against "TRIALS," "Every time I run up against "TRIBULATION," "I STOP," "And turned "OFF "BEAST "MODE, "BUT!!! "That's the time we need to be "Fighting, "To get back up, "That's the time to Turn Back on "BEAST" "MODE," "And! "No More "EXCUSES"..., "EXCUSES" ``Sound` ``Better`` to the one that's making them up, "Anybody that's "Determine to do something "Different, "Who wants something something "Different" in life, "It would "EVENTUALLY" be "DIFFERENT,"..."IF you "Change "Everything Around you, "Change The Way You "THINK," "Your "ENVIRONMENT," "Your "SURROUNDINGS,"... "And if you do "That".... "The wrong People that hang around you will all "Change "Also. (Hmmmmm) "But "Remember this "Though": "When you go to the "NEXT" "LEVEL" there's going to be a "NEW" "DEVIL"..., "NEW" "LEVELS".... "NEW" "DEVIL'S"..., "IT'S "The "Devil's Job, "To "Create` "CHALLENGES" for you, "OBSTACLE" "COURSES" And "ISSUES" And "CONFLICTS"...,in your way, "Only my "INSECURITIES," "MY "FEARS," " Sending people to talk to me out of my "Mission, "Cause he wants to try you, "And put you through the test, "But I can tell you now, "I ``PISS`` the `Devil` off "EVERYDAY," "BECAUSE, I'm like the "Energizer" "Bunny"... "I JUST WON'T STOP," "I Keep "GOING," "And "GOING" "And "GOING," "And if I "Quit or if I "Stop,... "All the pain that I went through, "Will be for "NOTHING," "NOW! "IF You know what you are "WORTH," "Then, "Go out "AND" "GET" what you're "WORTH," "But you gotta be "WILLING" to take the "HITS"..., "And Stop Calling your Friends and telling everybody, "That you're not where you want to be in life because of "Him or "Her,... "COWARDS"! do that, "And that ain't "ME" or "YOU"..., "I'M BETTER THAN "THAT,... "Tell" Yourself that every Morning, "When you look in the "Mirror," "And tell yourself, "That you're still "GIFTED," "I've been through some "PAIN," "But I'm still "GIFTED," "I "Buried` Some Loved Ones," "But

I'm still "GIFTED," I've had some "SETBACKS," "BUT" I'm still "GIFTED".... "I will find a "WAY! or I will make my own "WAY! "Because, "I am "STRONG" and "I WILL NOT GIVE UP MY DREAMS!!!... "I CAN! "I WILL! "I MUST!,... "I regret that I found all this out at the age of fifty-nine, "BUT" it ain't too "LATE! "And it ain't "OVER!... "I know now, "That I could've got a `Whole lot `More done in this Society that we're living in today, "I could have made more of a "DIFFERENCE," "This was my "MISSION," "To alarm the "YOUNGER" "GENERATION," "NOT" to "WASTE" "TIME," "Because, "When you look up, "You'll be 59-`Also, "So don't waits "TIME," "Because, "TIME" waits for no "MAN," and don't allow "FEAR" to come into play, "Because, "Fear" "KILLS" "DREAMS," `Alongside of "HATERS,".... "They would kill a `Ideal, or a `Good "DREAM or "VISION, "And you know "Why, "Because, "GOD" didn't show it to them, "HE" showed it to "YOU," `So if you want to "KILL a good "DREAM, "Tell it to a "SMALL "MINDED "PERSON," "That doesn't Understand the "FUTURE".....,"IF, "MARTIN "COOPER, `Would have listen to all his `NAYSAYERS` OR, all his "CRITICS," We would not have a "CELL "PHONE today, "He is the "INVENTOR" of the CELL PHONE, "BUT   he   had   a "DREAM".... "HE   had   a   "VISION," and "IF "PHILO "FARNSWORTH, "Who also was an `American "INVENTOR" and he was the investor of the "TELEVISION". He made a `CRUCIAL `CONTRIBUTION` to the early `DEVELOPMENT` of the `TELEVISION`,.... "IF "HENRY "FORD would have listened to anyone else other than his own "DREAMS and "VISIONS we will not have a "CAR" "Today, and, "IF "GARRETT" "MORGAN" would not have followed his "DREAMS" we would "NOT have the "TRAFFIC" "LIGHT" today, "What I'm trying to put out there, is "GOD" talks to you,`Through` your "DREAMS and "VISIONS to shows you the future,.... "DREAMS and VISIONS", we must learn how to "INTERPRET" them, "Some of our "Wildest "DREAMS" or "MESSAGES" from `SPIRIT` of "GOD `..... "That's how he does his

"COMMUNICATION" with us, "You see our "MINDS" are like ``BUTTERFLIES`` waiting to "METAMORPHOSIS" ourselves into a "HIGHER" "EXPRESSION" of "OURSELVES,"..... "NEW YEAR"..... "NEW ME"...... "NEW YEAR"...... "NEW ME,"..... I'm not going to "ALLOW" the habits of my past, "To stop me from my "METAMORPHOSIS," "A "TRANSFORMATION," "A ``POSSIBILITY`` of "CHANGE," and a "HIGHER" `Concept` of "MYSELF," "I want to "EVOLVE," get up off the ground, "And just stop eating "DIRT"....., "START CLIMBING my "LADDER" to "SUCCESS"......, "I have to be ``WILLING`` to do the "THINGS TODAY," "In order to have the "THINGS TOMORROW" that's why the "Book" of "Life" `Says, "The road to life is STRAIGHT and NARROW, and FEW there be that FIND it,.... "Because, "Few there will be, "That are "Willing to do the "Things "TODAY ``,"OTHERS `` won't "DO," "IN ORDER" to have the things "TOMORROW," "OTHERS" won't "HAVE,.... "You must take "REASONS ``,"And be "EXPLICIT" and "DESCRIPTIVE" in your "REASONS".... "Because your "REASONS `` have "POWER `` your "REASONS will "DRIVE" You.... "When you "DOUBT," "And when your face becomes "WEAK," your "REASONS" will "QUALIFY" your face, "When we're having that Inner "CONVERSATION" "Saying to you, "No don't do that, "Your "REASONS" will "BECOME" your "RIGHT HAND" and "Your "STAFF" "That will "COMFORT" you,... "IT would also "CONFLICT" you,...."To take you through those "CHALLENGING" "Moments,... "Wight down your "REASONS ``,"Why you want to be "SUCCESSFUL," "And read them "EVERYDAY,"... "That will make your "SUBCONSCIOUS" ``Mind "INTERACT" with your "CONSCIOUS" ``Mind`` sending "SUBLIMINAL MESSAGES" that will keep your "WILL" "Engaged," "By, giving your "MIND something to "THINK ABOUT" , "Because, "Your brain goes on "AUTOMATIC," "And start `Processing` `Information`, "So keep the window of "OPPORTUNITY" `OPEN` for `YOURSELF`, "And "MOTIVATE" "YOURSELF," "Not to think

"NEGATIVELY," or be "DEPRESSED," in any way,...... "And don't start hating somebody else over the wrong reasons, "Wanting Revenge with someone, "Just to get back at them," Wanting to beat yourself up, "Over losing the `Job `Opportunity, "You got to be willing to go against the "TIDE," "You got to be able to ``Harness your "WILL," "And say in spite of this, "I'm in "CONTROL "HERE, "I'm NOT GOING TO LET THIS TAKE ME OUT, "I'm not going to let this "DESTROY" me, "I'M COMING BACK," "And I'll be STRONGER, and "BETTER" because of it, "I will make a "DECLARATION," that this is what "I STAND FOR," I'm "STANDING" up for my "DREAMS," "I'm STANDING up for my "PEACE of MIND," "I'm standing up for my "HEALTH," "I want it, "And I'm `Going to `Go all out to `Get it, "It's not going to be easy, "BUT" when you want "CHANGE" ... "You can't send no one else to do it for you, "You have to do it "YOURSELF,"...... "GO" "GET" "IT".......(HMMMMMMMMM)

BY: DANIEL LAWRENCE JOHNSON

9 798888 120712